# Android®

## Fully Loaded

# Android®
# Fully Loaded

Rob Huddleston

Wiley Publishing, Inc.

# Android® Fully Loaded

Published by:
**Wiley Publishing, Inc.**
111 River Street
Hoboken, NJ 07030-5774
www.wiley.com

Copyright © 2011 by Wiley Publishing, Inc.

Published by Wiley Publishing, Inc., Indianapolis, Indiana
Published simultaneously in Canada

ISBN: 978-0-470-93002-1

Manufactured in the United States of America

10 9 8 7 6 5 4 3 2 1

For general information on our other products and services or to obtain technical support, please contact our Customer Care department within the U.S. at (800) 762-2974, outside the U.S. at (317) 572-3993 or fax (317) 572-4002.

Wiley also publishes its books in a variety of electronic formats. Some content that appears in print may not be available in electronic books. For more information about Wiley products, please visit our web site at www.wiley.com.

Library of Congress Control Number: 2010935567

# Acknowledgments

No technical book should be trusted that does not have a good tech editor backing up the author, but in the case of this book, I can say without question that it could not even have been written without the tech editor, Phil Nickinson. Phil is the editor at Android-Central.com, the online resource for all things Android and a site that all readers should bookmark and visit regularly. He is a pretty busy guy, between blogging, responding to forum posts, traveling to mobile device launches, and most importantly, taking care of his family. Editing a book like this was not, I think, high on his list of things to add to his plate, but he graciously agreed to do so nonetheless. True, I suspect he only agreed because he and I are cousins, but whatever the reason, I am in his debt. So my thanks to Phil and also to Shannon for letting me monopolize more of her husband's time and to Mia for letting me make her daddy busier. Phil also became a father again while we worked on this book. Welcome to the family, Bella.

Speaking of family, I am as always thankful to Kelley, Jessica, and Xander for their love and continued support for my writing and odd schedule. Thanks as well to my mom and dad for your support and for always being willing to hop on a plane to visit and help out with the grandkids.

The people at Wiley continue to be a wonderful group with whom to work. I've now had the pleasure to work with Stephanie McComb on two books, and I look forward to even more going forward. Thanks for being so kind and supportive, and for lunch. Kelly Henthorne did a great job editing, and Debbie Abshier and David Sechrist pulled everything together to produce the beautiful book you hold in your hands.

# Credits

**Senior Acquisitions Editor**
Stephanie McComb

**Editorial Director**
Robyn B. Siesky

**Vice President &
Executive Group Publisher**
Richard Swadley

**Vice President &
Executive Publisher**
Barry Pruett

**Business Manager**
Amy Knies

**Marketing Manager**
Sandy Smith

**Production Editor, Copy Editing,
Layout, Design, Proofreading,
and Indexing**
Abshier House

**Cover Image**
Michael E. Trent

# About the Author

Rob Huddleston has been developing Web pages and applications since 1994 and has been an instructor since 1999, teaching Web and graphic design to thousands of students. His clients have included the U.S. Bureau of Land Management, the U.S. Patent and Trademark Office, the States of California and Nevada, and many other federal, city, and county agencies; the United States Army and Air Force; Fortune 500 companies such as AT&T, Bank of America, Wells Fargo, Safeway, and Coca-Cola; software companies including Adobe, Oracle, Intuit, and Autodesk; the University of California, San Francisco State University, and the University of Southern California; and hundreds of small businesses and nonprofit agencies, both in the United States and abroad.

Rob is an adjunct professor in the Interactive Media program at the Art Institute of California, Sacramento. He is an Adobe Certified Instructor, Certified Expert, and Certified Developer, serves as an Adobe User Group Manager, and has been named as an Adobe Community Professional for his volunteer work answering user questions in online forums. He also helps users as an expert moderator on Adobe's Community Help system. Rob lives in Northern California with his wife and two children.

Rob is the author of *XML: Your visual blueprint™ for building expert websites using XML, CSS, XHTML, and XSLT; HTML, XHTML and CSS: Your visual blueprint™ for designing effective websites; Master VISUALLY: Dreamweaver CS4 and Flash CS4 Professional; ActionScript 3: Your visual blueprint™ for creating interactive projects in Flash CS4 Professional;* the *Adobe Flash Catalyst CS5 Bible,* and *Teach Yourself VISUALLY Web Design.* You can visit Rob's blog at www.robhuddleston.com or follow him on Twitter at twitter.com/robhuddles.

# Contents

# PART III: WORKING AND PLAYING 151

## Chapter 12: Documents 153

## Chapter 13: Games 165

## Chapter 14: Other Cool Apps    179

## Chapter 15: Advanced Topics    195

# INDEX    203

# Introduction

Adobe MAX is a conference sponsored by Adobe every year to bring together developers and designers who work with Adobe technologies and enable them to learn new techniques, network with one another, and, in general, get excited about the company and its products. Of course, the attendees of a conference like MAX are almost by definition geeks: These are folks who pay thousands of dollars and in some cases travel halfway around the world to attend. Like all large conferences, MAX kicks off every year with a lavishly produced keynote address, and being a conference populated primarily by geeks, you should not be surprised to discover that many attending the keynote use social media networks like Twitter to breathlessly report every announcement.

I have attended MAX, with a few exceptions, each year since 2005, and have noticed an interesting shift amongst the attendees during the keynote. Even two years ago, the crowd would have been lit by an almost unearthly blue glow from all of the people with open laptops. This year, however, few laptops were to be seen. This did not signal a shift away from social media use, but instead a shift in the devices being used. I would suspect that more people actually tweeted during the keynote than in the past, simply because more people use Twitter today than two years ago. The difference was that almost everyone in the theater was using a mobile phones.

MAX itself has recognized this shift: There is no question that the primary focus of the event is mobile development. A great many of the sessions focus on developing for mobile devices, and the conference's main sponsors have shifted from Internet firms like Yahoo to mobile providers. In fact, the two biggest sponsors at MAX this year were Motorola and BlackBerry, both of whom actually gave away phones to attendees; Motorola in fact went so far as to give every person at the conference — close to 5,000 in all — a new Droid 2.

MAX is something of a microcosm, but in many ways, it really reflects a tectonic shift in the bigger world as well. Even five years ago, the term "smartphone" was still new; if you had one, you were likely to be the focus of a lot of discussion. Today, the discussion has shifted from "is that a smartphone?" to "what smartphone is that?"

Smartphones have created a massive shift in how we interact online. Today, most people visiting the top sites on the Web still use desktop and laptop computers, but that trend is quickly changing. In fact, estimates are that by 2013, smartphones actually will surpass traditional computers to become the primary means by which we get online.

Smartphone technology also has opened up a new world for developers, providing an exciting and rapidly expanding market for applications built for mobile devices, providing you, the end user, a seemingly limitless supply of apps that will increase your productivity by enabling you to check e-mail, read and edit documents, view presentations, and much more — all on your phone. At least as many apps exist to decrease your productivity as well: No shortage of games exist to allow you to kill time and drain your battery while having fun.

I assume you are buying this book because you recently bought an Android-based smartphone. You hold in your hand a miniature computer; a computer so far advanced from those that took us to the moon that it is almost unfair to label both with that same term, computer. Certainly, referring to it as a phone at all is even misleading.

In some ways, carrying a device with that kind of speed and capabilities can be a bit daunting. Hopefully, reading through this book will help strip away some of that mystery, will help you better understand your new device, and will enable you to truly leverage all that it can do.

Most of all, please enjoy your new device.

# PART I

# The Basics

# Android Basics

## The Skim

About a month ago, I took my parents to see "Star Trek: The Exhibition" at the Sacramento Aerospace Museum. The exhibition is a museum piece celebrating the iconic sci-fi series. In addition to the normal array of props, costumes, and ship models, it has a series of displays on how *Star Trek* impacted real-world science and technology. Although things like transporters and warp drives are, unfortunately, likely impossible, Star Trek did directly inspire developers at Motorola in the creation of the first cell phones. Characters on the show also carried around small, portable computers called PADDs. As visionary as the show was, however, even they did not envision a world in which those portable communicators would merge with PADDs into a single device.

In many ways, we are at the dawn of a new age in computers. Our children will marvel at the thought of carrying around a device that can *only* make calls. My kids, in fact, are already used to the idea that Daddy's phone can take pictures, provide voice-guided directions, and, most importantly in their 8- and 4-year-old minds, allow them to play games.

3

Modern mobile devices really are nothing less than portable computers with all of the power — and complexity — that that implies. This chapter is designed to get you started using your Android device and understanding its key features.

## WHICH VERSION OF ANDROID DO I HAVE?

Android is an operating system like Windows or Mac OS. Well, honestly, it's a bit more like iOS, which runs the iPhone, iPod touch, and iPad, because like iOS, Android has been specifically designed to run on mobile devices. Today, dozens of smartphones run on Android, as do other types of devices, including tablet computers, e-readers — even microwave ovens.

Like all software, Android has undergone a series of revisions, with Google pushing out new versions of the software on a regular basis. Also like all software, each version is referred to by both a formal version number and a less formal code name or nickname. To date, all of the nicknames for Android have been pastries and other tasty snacks. (Google must not feed its developers well.)

The first publicly released version of Android, version 1.1, was made available on February 9, 2009. First-generation Android-based phones, such as the G1 for T-Mobile, initially were based on version 1.1.

In April 2009, Google released Android 1.5, otherwise known as Cupcake. It was followed in September 2009 by Donut, or version 1.6. Both of these updates introduced exciting new features, such as a video camera and improved market experience.

A little over a month after the release of Donut came Éclair, Android 2.0, which very

quickly was followed by 2.0.1. Also code-named Éclair, version 2.1 followed shortly thereafter in January 2010. Éclair added a ton of new features, all of which required significant improvements in the hardware on the phones running it, which is the polite way of saying that Éclair represented the point at which Google left early adopters, like myself, behind, as first-generation phones like my G1 would not be able to support 2.0 or future updates.

As of this writing, the most recent version of Android is version 2.2, nicknamed FroYo. For those of us who aren't as obsessed with sweets as the folks at Google, FroYo is the trade name for frozen yogurt. FroYo increases the speed and memory capabilities of Android and adds some exciting new features such as the ability to store applications on your device's memory card, and USB tethering, which allows you to use your phone's 3G data connection as a wireless hotspot for your computer's laptop. The market has seen a rush in new applications built specifically for FroYo, including Adobe's Flash Player, which enables those with this version of the OS to surf the actual Web.

In addition to these official versions, several so-called "flavors" of Android are available, offered by the various device manufacturers. Currently, four such flavors of Android exist. Vanilla or "stock" Android is the version officially offered by Google and runs on Google's own Nexus One phone, the Motorola Droid, and a few others. Devices with this flavor often receive major upgrades such as the latest version of the operating system before those with the other flavors. HTC, one of the leading manufacturers of Android devices, has a flavor known as Sense that adds a lot of custom home screen widgets. The Droid Eris, Droid Incredible, and Evo devices currently ship with HTC Sense. The other leading device manufacturer, Motorola, installs a custom version on many of its phones, including the Droid X and Droid 2. Finally, Samsung offers TouchWiz as its customized flavor of Android on many of its devices.

## SETTING UP YOUR ANDROID PHONE

When you first purchase a new phone, the salesperson likely will take you through the process of setting up your phone. Most of the steps are things that she needs to do, such as creating your account with the wireless provider. The final few steps, however, will be done by you. The most important of these is either setting up a Google account or logging into your existing e-mail and social networking accounts.

## GETTING A GOOGLE ACCOUNT

You need an account with Google in order to use most of the services available on Android. (Don't worry, you can still use a different kind of e-mail if you want.) The account is free and takes only a few moments to set up. If you already have a Google account, you can skip this section and move on to the fun stuff that follows.

You will be able to set up a Google account directly on your phone when you get it, but you can also do it in advance on your computer. Go to Google's home page, and move your mouse over the seemingly blank area at the top of your screen to make the site's additional menu items appear. On the top-right corner, you'll see

a link that says "Sign in," which you can click to go to the page that allows you to create your account. On this page, click the "Create an account now" link to proceed. The sign-up form is fairly straightforward; unless you've been living on Mars for the last decade or so, I'm sure you've filled out a dozen or so forms like this before. You need to provide a current e-mail address and create a password. Google has a cool little widget that tells you how strong your password is; because this password will be the gatekeeper for all of your Google information, including a lot of data you will get from your phone, you want to make it as strong as possible.

The next set of options on the form isn't terribly relevant to setting up your phone. Personally, I do use Google as my desktop browser's home page, but nothing bad will happen if you elect not to. Your location and birthday are in there, as far as I can figure, so that Google can collect demographic data on its customers. I've had a Google account for many years, and they've never sent so much as a card on my birthday. The word verification is needed to make it more difficult for spammers to create accounts. You can read the "Terms of Service" (TOS) if you want, but I suspect that it is just a bunch of legal mumbo jumbo; I know I've never read a TOS in my life. Click "I accept. Create my account," and you're done.

## SYNCHING YOUR PHONE WITH YOUR ACCOUNT

After you have your phone unpackaged and charged and you've created your Google account, you can synchronize the two. This will give your phone access to the same data as you have on your computer; for example,

## WHAT MAKES A GOOD PASSWORD?

A good, strong password protects your data in the same way a good, strong deadbolt protects your house. The first rule in making a good password is to pick something that has nothing at all to do with you personally. A very common method of trying to get someone's password is a method known as "social engineering." Many people pick passwords that relate to their personal life in some way — a child's or spouse's name, the name of a pet, an anniversary date or birthday, or something similar. Keep in mind that in these days of hyper-connectivity, a person doesn't need to know you to get this data, as it can be gleaned from Facebook, other social networking sites, or even by simply doing a search on your name. If the obvious passwords don't work, the next thing the hacker will try to do is known as a brute-force attack. I'm sure you've seen movies in which the barbarian hordes try to beat down the castle gates with a battering ram, the theory being that even the strongest gates eventually will crack if you hit them repeatedly enough times. Brute-force password attacks work on the same theory, only with fewer sweaty, foul-smelling soldiers and less blood. Instead of a battering ram, the hacker uses a computer program that simply keeps entering passwords until it stumbles across the right one. Although a truly determined hacker might try every possible combination of letters, most will instead rely on dictionaries, starting with "a" and going through "zythum," or something along those lines. The best defense against a brute-force attack is to make sure that your password is not a real word at all, so that it won't appear in that dictionary list. Longer passwords are better than short ones; it's also better if you use some lowercase and uppercase letters and use the character keys on your keyboard as well. If the dictionary attack fails, the hacker might actually try using all combinations of these characters, but some straightforward math reveals how longer passwords help defend against this. There are 308,915,776 possible combinations of the 26 letters in the English alphabet, but if you add in mixed cases, numbers, and the other characters, that number jumps to 646,990,183,449 possibilities. Add just two more characters, and the number of possibilities shoots all the way up to 5,595,818,096,650,401. The point here is that it is going to be a lot harder to hack a password when it is one of several quadrillion choices, rather than one of several hundred million.

if you choose to use Gmail, Google's e-mail service, you will be able to use it from either your phone or your computer. This synchronization is very easy: simply enter your Google username, which will be the e-mail address you used when you registered for the account, and your password into your phone and then give the service a minute or so to do its magic. Note that some people who have had accounts with Google for a long time might have a distinct username, rather than an e-mail address.

## ACCESSORIES

With Android sales rising rapidly, more and more accessories are becoming available all the time. Following is a list of some of the most essential accessories to consider purchasing. You can find many of these accessories at the same store where you purchased your phone or online at sites such as www.androidcentral.com.

◇ Car charger (see Figure 1.1). You are likely going to want to invest in a car charger to keep the phone charged while you drive. This is particularly important if you're going to use Navigation, the turn-by-turn GPS directions application (see Chapter 6 for details on Navigation). Navigation is one of the truly awesome applications available, particularly because it is free, but it will drain your battery very quickly, so I always make sure to keep my phone plugged in when I use

Navigation. Android devices charge via a USB port, so car chargers may be interchangeable between them. Unfortunately, almost all current devices have moved from a mini USB port to a smaller and appropriately named micro USB port, so my G1 charger would not work with my Droid X, but the Droid X charger works fine with my wife's LG Ally Android phone.

◇ Screen protectors (see Figure 1.2). Your screen really is your phone, and if it becomes too scratched or damaged, you will not be able to use your phone at all. Thus, invest immediately in some screen protectors. These clear plastic sheets stick to your screen and absorb all of the scratches and a lot of the other abuse your phone is likely to endure. When one becomes too scratched, simply peel it off and apply another. Just be sure to carefully

Figure 1.1
A car charger with the micro USB connector

Figure 1.2
A set of screen protectors; be sure to buy a brand designed specifically for your model of phone.

Figure 1.3
A standard set of headphones that I use to listen to my phone

clean the screen before applying the protector, or else you will end up with unsightly bubbles.

◇ Headphones (see Figure 1.3) or Blue-tooth device (see Figure 1.4). In 2009, California adopted a law making it illegal to talk on your phone while driving unless you used a hands-free device of some kind. Many states and other jurisdictions are following suit, so this accessory can be seen more as a legal requirement. Keep in mind, though, that you will not only be talk-ing on your phone, as your Android

device also will be your MP3 player, podcast player, in-car navigation system, and much more. All of these require that you be able to hear the phone, which in turn requires a head-set or Bluetooth device. The Droid X includes a standard headphone jack, so any headphones you already own for your MP3 player or other devices will work, at least for listening to music and movies. However, you will need some other device — likely a Bluetooth headset — in order to talk into your phone without holding it.

◇ Car mount (see Figure 1.5). This device allows you to mount your phone on your dashboard, which can be very

Figure 1.4
A Bluetooth headset

Figure 1.5
A car mount for the Droid X

helpful when using Navigation and when using the phone as an alternative to your car stereo. When you insert your phone into the car mount, it switches to a special car mode. For more details on Car mode and using the car mount, see Chapter 7. Your car mount may include a car charger.

◇ Extra storage (see Figure 1.6). Most phones today include the ability to add storage with a MicroSD memory card. As the name implies, these cards are similar to the larger SD card you already may be using for your digital camera, only smaller. Your device

Figure 1.6
The 16GB MicroSD card, on the left, came preinstalled in my Droid X. The 8GB SD card on the right is shown for scale.

will almost certainly have a MicroSD card in it when you purchase, but you should check to see whether you can replace it with one with a larger capacity.

◇ Protective case (see Figure 1.7). A protective case may reduce damage if the phone is dropped. I have a soft gel that wraps around the back of the phone and has the advantage of being very easy to remove, which is handy because I cannot place the phone in the car mount with the case on.

◇ Micro USB cable (see Figure 1.8). One of these cables should have come with your phone, but as you will need this cable to charge your phone as well as connect it to your computer to transfer files, you may want one or two extras. I keep one plugged into the wall charger, another plugged into the computer, and a third in the bag with my laptop, thus ensuring that I will be able to plug my phone in just about anywhere.

Figure 1.7
A soft gel case, one of many styles available

Figure 1.8
A micro USB cable

## THE HOME SCREEN

The home screen in Android is like the desktop on your computer (see Figure 1.9). It provides a place for you to place shortcuts to your favorite and most-used applications. You can also customize your home screen with widgets for applications that display the time, up-to-the-minute stock quotes or sports scores, the song you currently are listening to, Google search, and much more. You can set the background to anything you like. See Chapter 2 for information on adding shortcuts and widgets to your home screen.

You can access the home screen any time on your phone by pressing the Home button. All Android phones include a button on the phone itself, usually with an icon representing a house, to go to the home screen. Figure 1.10 shows this button on a Google G1 phone, and Figure 1.11 shows it on a Motorola Droid X, and Figure 1.12 on the Motorola Cliq.

The home screen actually is composed of several different screens. Older phones such as the G1 had three screens, while newer models such as the Droid X have as many as seven, depending on the flavor of Android your device runs. Each of these

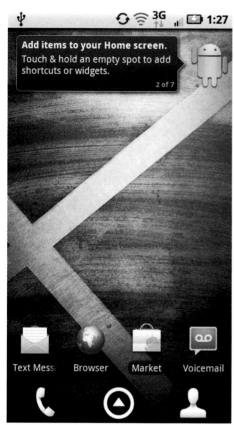

Figure 1.9
The default main home screen on the Droid X

Figure 1.11
The Home button on the Droid X

Figure 1.12
The Home button on the Cliq

Figure 1.10
The Home button on the G1

screens works the same as each of the others, providing a place to put shortcuts and widgets. You can move between screens by sliding your finger to the right or left. Some phones also provide small icons you can use to quickly access your other screens.

See Chapter 3 for more details on customizing and working with your home screen.

## THE APPLICATIONS LAUNCHER

You are likely to have more applications than can fit on your home screen, so Android provides the Applications Launcher to store the rest of them. On most phones, the launcher can be accessed by tapping the button found at the bottom of the screen (see Figure 1.13). The launcher automatically lists all of your installed applications alphabetically. You can scroll through them by simply sliding your finger up on the screen. Touch an application to launch it. Unlike the home screen, the launcher does not provide any customization, so you cannot rearrange or even rename applications.

## THE NOTIFICATION BAR

The top of your Android screen is the Notification Bar, an area where the operating system and applications give you alerts and let you know what is going on. One side of the bar is reserved for applications, and the other is an area for applications to run. Table 1.1 shows some of the more common icons you will find on the bar. Note that you will not see these icons all of the time, and some of them will occasionally show up while a process is running, so unless you happen to glance at your screen at the right moment, you may not see it at all. Also, you may install additional applications that add their own notification icons.

If you need to see details for your notifications, you can pull the Notification Bar down. Simply press your finger anywhere on the bar and drag down to expand it to fit your screen. Depending on the applications you have running, you should see details of the notifications, such as the number of applications that need updating or the number of unread e-mail messages you have waiting.

## PHONE SETTINGS

This is an area where you can customize much of the functionality on the phone, very

**Table 1.1**

Common Android Notification Icons

| Icon | What it Means |
| --- | --- |
| | An alarm is on. |
| | Bluetooth is active on your phone. |
| | Bluetooth device is connected. |
| | GPS is active. |
| | Wi-Fi is active. |
| | An application is currently downloading. |
| | The phone is set to vibrate. |
| | Sounds are turned off. |
| | Network strength is indicated. |
| 3G | You are connected to a 3G network. |
| | Your phone is in Airplane mode. |
| | Your phone is synching with Google's servers. |
| | You are connected via USB to a computer. |
| | Battery is full. |
| | Battery is partially full. |
| | Battery is charging. |
| | An application has finished downloading and installing. |
| | You are currently making a call. |
| | You have voice mail. |
| | You have an unread text message. |
| | Phone is connected to a car mount. |
| | Connection for Media Share is detected. |
| | Application updates are available. |

Figure 1.13
The Applications Launcher

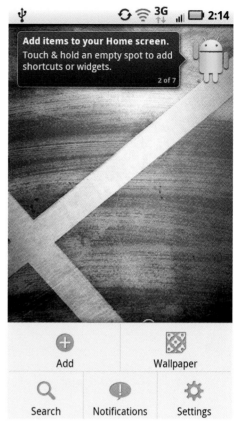

Figure 1.14
Getting to Settings from the home screen

similar to the way you can use the Windows Control Panel to customize your PC.

On most phones, you can access the settings by pressing your phone's Menu button while on the home screen (see Figure 1.14). Settings is also an installed application, available in the Applications Launcher. When you dig into specific settings, you can use your phone's Back button to return to the previous screen.

The precise options available in the settings will vary slightly from one phone to the next and even from one carrier to

the next, but in general, they contain the same basic groups of settings, as shown in Table 1.2.

Other devices may include additional settings. For example, the Droid X also includes an HDMI settings screen for connecting your device to a high-definition television or projector. See Chapter 9 for more details on this feature. Verizon includes a feature on its service plans called Backup Assistant to help back up your phone's data, so Verizon's phones also include a settings widget for it.

Table 1.2
Settings Categories

| Category | General Uses |
|---|---|
| Wireless & Networks | Allows access to turn Wi-Fi on and off and configure settings to allow the phone to connect to (or serve as) Wi-Fi hotspots, as well as Bluetooth settings and other mobile networks. |
| Call Settings | From here, you can set up your voice mail, configure call forwarding and call waiting and other options relating to using your phone as a phone. See Chapter 3 for details on using your phone as, well, as a phone. |
| Sound & Display | Set ringtones, notification sounds, and volume. You can also configure the screen's brightness and how long the screen will stay on. |
| Data Manager | Use these controls to configure which applications can remain synchronized with online services. |
| Location & Security | Set your location and manage security settings such as requiring pattern input to unlock your phone. |
| Accounts | Manage your Google, social networking, and carrier-specific accounts. |
| Battery Manager | Included on some newer devices, the Battery Manager allows you to set up profiles and manage power usage to maximize your battery life. |
| Search | Customize Google search settings. |
| Applications | See a complete list of applications and how much space they are taking. You can also uninstall applications from here or force them to close if they stop working. |
| SD Card & Phone Storage | Mounts or unmounts the SD card to allow access to it from a desktop computer and enables you to see how much space you have left. |
| Date & Time | Set the formats for date and time display. |
| Language & Keyboard | Controls the language and regional settings of the phone. |
| Accessibility | Enable options to make your phone easier to use if you have a disability such as reduced hearing or vision or a mobility impairment. |
| Text-to-Speech | Set up text-to-speech options, used by applications such as Navigation to translate driving directions into speech. |
| About Phone | Find out which version of Android you are using, what applications are chewing up your battery, and, if you really want to, read a bunch of legalese about Android. |

# WIRELESS AND NETWORK SETTINGS

Your phone has a wide variety of controls to deal with wireless connectivity. You can access these controls from your phone's Settings application. See the previous section for details on getting to the settings, but when there, select the first option: Wireless & Networks.

The first option in this screen turns Airplane mode on or off, which disables all connections into and out of your phone (see Figure 1.15). As its name implies, it is designed for when you are in an airplane. Airplane mode is important because in the United States, it is illegal to have your phone turned on and potentially transmitting data while the plane you are in is in flight. Although the actual science behind whether or not a phone could interfere with a plane and bring it down is still a matter of debate, the law is clear. Generally, your phone needs to be completely powered off during takeoff and until the plane reaches 10,000 feet and then again once the plane descends below 10,000 feet until it lands. Between those times, however, you can use your phone to listen to music, play games, or watch movies — any of the activities you can do without data connections. By the way, if a flight attendant tells you to turn off your phone even above 10,000 feet and even when it is in Airplane mode, I would suggest that you do so. It really is not worth having to spend your time talking to Homeland Security when you land.

The next setting available is a simple toggle that enables you to turn Wi-Fi on or off. When I purchased my first Android phone, the Google G1, I asked the T-Mobile salesman what the heck 3G was, because it

Figure 1.15
The phone with Airplane mode enabled. The signal indicator displays an airplane when this mode is enabled.

seemed to be one of those terms that people like to throw around but actually have no idea what it really is. I don't honestly think he did, either, but he gave me a plausible answer nonetheless: 3G provides, in his words, "high-speed-like connections to the phone." What does "high-speed-like" mean, exactly? Well, in short, it means that you are not getting actual high-speed Internet access, but if you are old enough to remember surfing the Web on 56K modems, it is not quite that slow. In practice, it turns out

15

## TIDBIT

3G is all the rage right now for people marketing mobile devices. If you watch TV at all, you likely have seen the commercials by AT&T and Verizon in which they each try to claim that they have more or better or faster 3G coverage. However, some inquiring minds might wonder whether there was ever a 1G or 2G. The answer, in short, is yes. 3G is defined, rather dryly, by Wikipedia as "International Mobile Telecommunications-2000 (IMT — 2000), better known as 3G or 3rd Generation, as a generation of standards for mobile phones and mobile telecommunications services fulfilling specifications by the International Telecommunication Union." So 3G actually stands for "3rd Generation," which, of course, means that there must have been a 1st and 2nd generation. 1G was, in fact, the mobile technology used by the first mobile phones in the 1980s. It is worth noting, however, that the 1G moniker was applied only to these phones in retrospect after 2G was adopted in the early 1990s. Neither was really exciting enough to be worth advertising about, which is why 3G was the first one that anyone ever heard about. 4G, by the way, already is being rolled out by Sprint, with Verizon to follow in 2011. T-Mobile has a pseudo-4G service called HSPA+.

Instead, if you are within range of a Wi-Fi connection, you can switch over to that and get true high speed. This also can be nice if you have, for example, an old G1 phone that is no longer connected to a wireless provider's plan. Using Wi-Fi, you can still surf the Internet, play games, listen to music, and download new applications. Thanks to this, my old phone has now become a gaming device for the kids.

To connect to a Wi-Fi network, you need to not only turn Wi-Fi on, but you also need to tell your phone that you want to connect to a network by selecting Wi-Fi. These settings display all of the networks in range of your phone and their relative signal strength. Figure 1.16 shows the networks available at my house. The Serenity network is my home Wi-Fi, and you can see I have a very strong signal but that the network is secure. The others are, I assume, my neighbors' networks. If I select a secure network to which I am not connected, I will be prompted to enter the key code for that network. Assuming I enter the correct code, my phone will connect to that network and then remember it, automatically connecting any time it comes in range. When I select a network to which I am connected, I can see status information for that network. Remembered networks also will display on the main list of networks even if they are not in range. Press and hold on a network and you'll get an option to "forget" it.

Press your phone's Back button to return to the Wireless & Network Settings screen, where you can enable Bluetooth and configure the settings using the next two controls on the main Wireless Settings screen. In order to use a Bluetooth headset, you need

to be somewhere in between most of the time. However, your phone does not have to use 3G at all if you do not want it to.

**Figure 1.16**
The Wi-Fi networks available at my house

to enter its name, although if you select the Scan for Devices control, your phone automatically will discover the headset. See Chapter 4 for more details on setting up and using Bluetooth.

Many corporate networks allow employees to access protected internal network documents using a Virtual Private Network (VPN). Assuming you have proper access to a VPN, you can use the VPN settings screen, accessible from the main Wireless & Network Settings screen to configure your connection. If you do not know how to con-

nect to your VPN, contact your company's IT department.

The Mobile Networks settings allow you to control what happens when you leave your carrier provider's coverage area. Be aware that many providers charge handsomely for the privilege of using your phone outside their coverage area. In 2009, I had the opportunity to teach a class on Grand Cayman island and discovered that my carrier at the time was going to charge me more than $1 per minute just to have my phone on and connected to some foreign network. That cost did not include the cost of making any calls. Data charges were even worse, at $1.50 per megabyte. The Web is full of horror stories of people traveling abroad and returning home to cell phone bills in the thousands of dollars. You can avoid these charges by setting your phone to the Home only option in the settings. When I was in the Caymans, I kept my phone in Airplane mode, just to be on the safe side.

## RINGTONES

Ringtones can be a highly personal and, of course, highly annoying, feature of your phone. Android phones allow you to set a default ringtone from one of about a few dozen choices out of the box. Later, when you have music uploaded to your phone, you can use those songs as your ringtone, which is discussed in Chapter 7. You also can set specific ringtones for specific people, which is covered in Chapter 3. For now, we want to look at setting a default ringtone.

In the main Settings screen, select Sound & Display. Then select Phone ringtone. A list of the default ringtones will display. Touch each in turn to listen to it. When you find one you like, tap OK. Back on the Sound &

17

Display Settings screen, you can set the volume of the ringtone using Ringer volume; simply slide your finger along the slider to increase or decrease the volume.

Another important default sound is the Notification ringtone, which is the sound that plays whenever your phone or an application wants to let you know that something is happening. Like the call ringtone, you can select from a list of default notification sounds, or you can further customize it using third-party applications.

## SILENCING YOUR PHONE

Although I am sure that you have never forgotten to turn off your ringer when sitting in an important meeting, you, of course, know people who have. On Android, you have a few methods by which you can silence your phone. The easiest method, only available on most (but not all) newer devices, is to use the slider on the phone's lock screen (see Figure 1.17).The easiest way to get to the lock screen is to press the power button once to dim the phone and then again to wake it. (Don't worry, you're not actually turning it off.)

If your phone is not already asleep, you can go into the Sound & Display settings and tap the first option: Silent mode. A quicker method, though, is available anywhere on your phone: press and hold the power button for 2–3 seconds. On the Droid X, this button is located on top of the phone. Other older models may use the End Call button (if there is one). You will see a menu appear that enables you to silence your phone or, if it is already silenced, turn the sound back on. This menu also allows you to quickly enter and exit Airplane mode.

Phones that are running Android 2.1 or below can be silenced by pressing the volume-down button repeatedly, which cycles through the different volume levels (the Droid X has 15 of them), through vibrate mode, and finally to silent mode. This function was removed in Android 2.2.

Newer phones such as the Droid X include a great feature known as the Smart Sensor to help keep you from embarrassing yourself by leaving the ringer on when you do not mean to. These settings are located at the very bottom of the Sound & Display

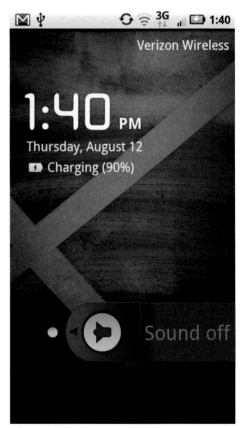

**Figure 1.17**
Silencing the phone from the Lock screen

settings. Unfortunately, neither of these settings is clearly explained on the phone. The first, Double-Tap to Silence, enables you to quickly silence the ringtone when a call comes in by double-tapping. It does not completely free you from the glares of your boss and co-workers, because the phone will likely begin ringing before you realize a call is coming in, but it will be the fastest way to shut the thing up. The second, Smart Profile: Face Down to Vibrate, lets you simply flip the phone over on its face to put it in vibration mode when an alert or call comes in.

## ORIENTATION AND THE ACCELEROMETER

The accelerometer is one of the coolest features of modern smartphones. Essentially, it is a device inside that phone that knows which direction the phone is moving. Some pretty cool games rely on the accelerometer, but so does a basic function of the phone. Although the normal way most people hold a phone lends itself to a portrait orientation, in which the screen is taller than it is wide, the accelerometer can let the phone reorient itself when you turn it in your hand, so that even if you hold it sideways, everything will still be right-side up. Although this has an obvious use when watching a wide-screen movie or video, it can often be helpful when simply reading a Web page or e-mail. I honestly can't think of a good reason to turn this off, but if you really want to, you can do so in the Screen & Display settings.

## LOCK YOUR PHONE

When you do not use your phone for more than a few minutes, it will save battery life by turning off the screen. Different

devices have different ways of waking it back up, mostly involving pressing one of the buttons, generally Home, on the phone. When you wake up the phone, you will need to unlock it by sliding the Unlock button (see Figure 1.18).

You always have to consider the possibility of losing your phone, or even just setting out somewhere where others could get into it, say on your desk at work. Android 2.2 introduces several new ways to security lock your phone. If you would like to prevent unauthorized use, you can lock the screen so that whenever you turn it back on, you

Figure 1.18
Unlocking the phone

need to enter a special pattern. You config-ure this feature by going into the Location & Security settings and then scrolling down and selecting Screen lock.

## Securing with a Pattern

From the Security settings, if neces-sary select Security lock type and then Pattern lock. If you use the pattern, you are presented with a screen that provides instructions. When you click Next, you see an example of what you need to do, which involves drawing something that connects at least four of the dots. When you click Next again, you can draw your own pattern. Click Continue, and you will have to draw your pattern again to make sure you know what it is. When you click Confirm, you will be taken back to the Settings screen. From here, you can set the Security lock timer, so you can control whether you need to enter

**TIP**

Your phone gives you five attempts at the pattern. After that, it locks itself down for 30 seconds. When this timeout is finished, you will see a "Forgot pattern?" button. Selecting this brings up a screen that allows you to unlock your phone by entering your Google username and password. When entered correctly, your phone will unlock and take you right to the pattern screen where you can create a new pattern that you will, at least hopefully, remember this time.

the pattern every time the monitor is off or only when the phone has been idle, with the screen off, for a set period of time.

The next time your phone's screen locks, you will need to provide the pattern again to unlock it. Should you decide at some point to remove this feature, return to the Set-tings screen and deselect the Security lock pattern option. Note that you will have to provide your pattern again in order to turn this feature off.

## Securing with a Passcode

The Droid X and other devices with Android 2.2 enable you to use a password instead of a pattern to lock the phone. You access the password settings using the same process as outlined previously for the pat-tern, but selecting Security & Location, Security Lock, Security Lock Type, and finally Passcode Lock. You are presented with a numeric grid that you can use to enter your passcode, which must be at least four digits. Type in the code you want to use and select the check mark in the lower-left corner. You need to enter the code a second time to confirm it. Then the next time your phone locks, you need to enter the passcode to unlock it.

## STORAGE

You can use the MicroSD card as addi-tional storage for the data on your phone. By default, any pictures or videos you take with the phone's camera will be stored on the card, as will application data such as your contacts and high scores on your games. If your device is running at least Android 2.2, you can even store some applications them-selves on the card, which is a great feature as older phones were often very limited in the number of applications you could install simply because the phone's internal storage was limited.

Every phone has a slightly different place to insert the MicroSD card, so you need to read the manual that came with your phone to find it (see Figure 1.19). If you are the type who likes to throw the manual away, unread, the very second you open the box, then you can find instructions online. Be aware that every phone has a limit as to how big of a card it can read, so be sure to check that before you waste money on a card that is too big for your phone.

After you have the card in your phone, you can transfer files to and from your computer. You simply need to plug the USB cable that came with your phone into a standard USB jack on your computer. You should see an icon appear on the Notification Bar telling you that the USB is connected. If you have it enabled, you also will hear the notification sound. Then pull down the Notification Bar from the top of the screen and select the USB Connection notification.

On the Droid X, you have four options as to how your device should connect to your computer (see Figure 1.20). Traditionally, you attach a smartphone to a computer and mount the SD card as a USB drive so that you can transfer files. This is a long-established technology and is widely supported across a wide range of devices, from desktop and laptop computers to modern car stereos and more. The downside to this system,

Figure 1.19
The Droid X MicroSD card is accessed by removing the back cover, then the battery.

**TIP**

You should avoid simply unplugging your phone from the USB cord when it is connected to the computer and using the USB Storage option, as this might cause the files on the card to become corrupt. Instead, you should eject the USB drive from your computer and then remount the smart card on your phone. The process of ejecting the drive differs depending on the operating system of your computer, but on most modern versions of Windows, you can right-click the USB icon on your task tray and select Eject. On a Mac, you generally can drag the drive's icon to the trash can. On your phone, you should go back to the same USB Settings menu you used to mount the drive originally and select Unmount.

though, is that while you have the card mounted on the computer, the device itself cannot read it, so for example, you would be unable to listen to music or view pictures stored on the card via the phone while you have it mounted. The Droid X supports this with its USB Mass Storage mode. However, the Droid X and a few other newer phones also support a new method, called PC mode, that actually allows for two-way communication, so both your computer and your phone retain full access to the card. The Windows Media Sync mode is intended to streamline synchronizing media files, such as music, between your computer and your device. Finally, Charge Only simply

lets your phone know that it is plugged in to charge the battery and that you do not intend to transfer files. This mode can be helpful when you plug the phone into a computer in a tightly restricted office environment that might disallow installing the necessary drivers or transferring files to your device.

At this point, if you are using Windows, you will get a dialog box on your machine asking how you want to deal with the new drive that suddenly appeared, because your computer may see your phone as an

Figure 1.20
Choosing the mode to use to connect to the computer

22

additional hard drive. The Droid X, when connected to a Windows 7 computer, displays a special Control Panel window that provides information about the phone and links to tasks such as synching media and transferring files. I generally select the Open folder to view files option to open Windows Explorer, at which point I can simply drag files from my computer's drive to the phone or vice versa. The procedure is essentially the same if you are on a Mac.

## TEXT INPUT

While some Android-based phones include a physical keyboard, all have an onscreen keyboard you can use. Typing on an onscreen keyboard can be a challenge, but after you get used to it, I think you'll find it fairly easy to use. My G1 was one of those phones that had a physical keyboard, and yet by the end of the time I used it, I found that I relied on the onscreen keyboard at least as often as I used the physical one.

The Language & keyboard settings screen provides you with some options to control your keyboard. From the main Settings screen, tap Language & keyboard, which will display the Text settings.

### Multitouch Keyboard

The Droid X ships with two possible text input methods: the multitouch keyboard or Swype. The default multitouch keyboard functions as a simple onscreen keyboard that will appear automatically whenever you are in a text field of some kind. You can select the arrow key in the lower-right corner for Shift, or the key below it to display numbers and special characters. Additional characters are available by tapping the Alt key.

The Text settings screen does provide a few additional settings for the multitouch keyboard. You can turn on vibration and sound for keypresses and enable auto-capitalization and auto-punctuation, both of which will save you a considerable number of taps when entering longer blocks of text. The keyboard also includes suggestions for words as you type and auto-correction.

If your phone has a physical keyboard, the onscreen keyboard will likely not appear if you have the physical keyboard out, so you need to be sure to keep the phone collapsed if you want to use the onscreen keyboard.

## Swype

The other input method provided by default on the Droid X is Swype, an application that greatly simplifies inputting text into your phone. You can enable Swype by selecting it as the input method.

Swype takes some getting used to, and you will need to practice a bit to fully get the hang of things. After you have it figured out, I suspect you will love it. Swype allows you to trace paths across the keyboard to spell words, rather than having to tap each letter individually (see Figure 1.21). As you trace the path, the software guesses what letters you wish to use and from that, guesses the word you are trying to spell. Saying that Swype is guessing might imply that it is not very accurate, but in fact, you will be surprised at how often it guesses correctly. When Swype is unsure, it prompts you with choices for words it thought you might be spelling.

As of this writing, the Droid X comes with Swype preinstalled. However, Swype should be available on an ever-increasing number of devices as time goes on, so if

## TIP

The Swype keyboard includes a quick, hands-on tutorial on its use. Long-press the key in the lower-left corner of the keyboard to display a Tips screen and then select Tutorial to access it. The Tutorial should take about 5 minutes to complete, and will show you how to do pretty much everything you need to do with the keyboard, along with allowing you to practice as you go. I found that I was quite comfortable using Swype almost immediately after completing the tutorial.

your phone does not yet support it, keep checking the Market and online blogs such as the one at http://androidcentral.com for details on its availability.

## PHONE INFORMATION

The main Settings page also includes an About Phone page. From here, you can check to see whether you are eligible to upgrade to a new version of Android, to check your phone's current status, and to find out the model number of your phone and which version of Android you are running.

## CHARGING

An unfortunate reality of all smart phones is that they tend to have a much shorter battery life than traditional mobile phones. Although each generation of smartphones can remain unplugged longer, you should plan to keep your phone plugged in

Figure 1.21

Tracing the word Google on the Swype keyboard

as much as possible. You have three primary ways you can charge your phone: a wall socket, car charger, and USB. Your phone will have come with a wall charger, so simply plug it into any standard outlet and plug the other end into your phone. The same applies to the car charger, which like other devices, charges off of what used to be the cigarette lighter but is in most modern cars simply a power outlet. USB charging is perhaps the nicest method, as you can charge your phone off of any computer with a USB plug. In fact, on many newer phones, the wall charger actually uses the same micro USB cable you rely on to connect and charge your phone off of your computer (see Figure 1.22). If you work in an environment with very tight computer restrictions whereby you cannot normally use USB devices, you need not worry; plugging the phone in to charge it does not necessarily mean you will be mounting the USB drive. You can, in fact, even charge your phone off a computer that is turned off, something I do frequently in hotels when I turn my laptop off to go to bed but keep my phone plugged into the computer and allow it to continue to charge. Charging off your computer is generally slower than charging off a wall outlet, so if you are in a hurry you should plug it into the wall.

The amount of time your phone takes to charge will vary from one model to the next, but in general, you should allow several hours of charging if you have completely depleted the battery. Likewise, the amount of time you can go without charging will vary depending not only on the model of phone you use but also on what applications you are running. Most phones should be able to go several days at least if you leave

them alone, but may hold only a few hours' charge if you use battery-intensive applications such as anything involving GPS or Bluetooth.

Figure 1.22
The stock wall charger that was included as the only accessory with the Droid X; the cable is a standard micro USB.

# Applications

## The Skim

Early cell phones were just that — phones. Later, their capabilities began to expand to include texting, and eventually they allowed users to play simple games, take pictures, or browse Web pages. Still, they were phones that could sort of act like computers. Today's smartphones, on the other hand, are portable computers, first and foremost. They just happen to be computers that can, almost incidentally, make phone calls.

## USING THE ANDROID MARKET

The Android Market is the primary resource to find applications for download. Although no requirement demands that developers use the Market, most will because of the visibility it provides their applications.

You can access the Market at any time using the application that comes preinstalled on your phone (see Figure 2.1). The main screen on the Market application allows you to browse through popular featured applications, browse apps or games, or search for applications.

The Apps tab brings up a new screen that displays categories of

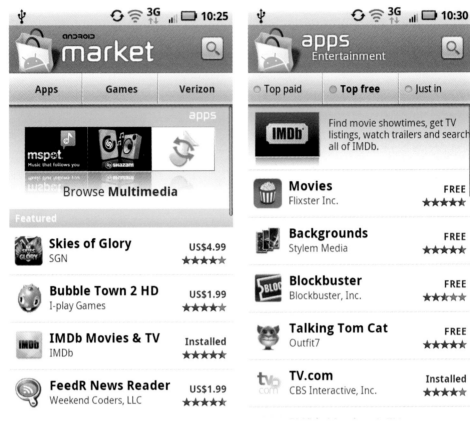

Figure 2.1
The Market main screen

Figure 2.2
A list of applications within a category

applications. Selecting one of these categories displays a list of the applications in that category. You can sort the list by Top paid, Top free, or Just in. Each application is listed by its name, the name of the developer, its cost, and its current user rating (see Figure 2.2).

Selecting an application brings up a page that shows the details of the application, screen shots, and user reviews (see Figure 2.3). At any point, you can use your phone's Back button to return to either the application list or the main screen of the Market.

## SEARCHING FOR APPLICATIONS

If you have a particular application in mind, you can use the Market's search feature to find it. From the Market's main screen, select the search icon. Type the name or keywords of the application you want to find and then select the magnifying glass icon to see a list of matching applications. As with browsing, the search list displays the name of the application, the name of the developer, the cost, and the rating of the application.

IMDb is the world's largest collection of movie, TV and celebrity information.
-Find Showtimes
-Watch trailers
-Browse photos
-Get TV listings
-Track DVD/Blu-ray releases
-Explore popular charts – award winners, IMDb top 250, etc.
-Search over 1.5 million movies and TV shows

Version 1.0  635KB

Install

Figure 2.3
An application's information screen

## DOWNLOADING AND INSTALLING FREE APPLICATIONS

Many of the applications you will find in the market are free. In fact, the Android Market has a higher percentage of free applications than any other mobile application marketplace, due in large part to the fact that Google imposes a much smaller initial fee for developers than some of its competitors do. When you find a free application that interests you, select the Install button at the bottom of the application's detail page. Your phone then will display a

message page detailing what services on the phone the application will need access to (see Figure 2.4). Press OK, and the application will begin downloading.

You are taken back to your most recent search or browse page, and the Notification Bar will display an icon letting you know that the application is downloading. The Notification Bar will inform you after the download is complete, at which point you can select the application to launch it (see Figure 2.5).

## PAYING FOR APPLICATIONS

If you decide to download an application that requires payment, you can purchase it directly through your phone. Go to the page for the application and select Buy. As with free applications, the download process for paid apps begins with an information screen letting you know what services the applica-

### TIP

You can link a credit card to your Google account to simplify the process of purchasing applications. After it is linked, the card will display directly on the checkout screen, so you do not have to keep entering information over again. Entering these linked cards involves going to http://checkout.google.com, logging in with your Google account, and then entering the credit card information on the screen provided.

29

> **TIP**
>
> You can get a full refund on any application purchased through the Android Market within 24 hours of that purchase. To return an application and get a refund, go to the Downloads section of the Market (usually by pressing the Menu button), select the application, and select Uninstall & refund. If you only see an Uninstall button, then you are either looking at a free app or your 24-hour period has expired.

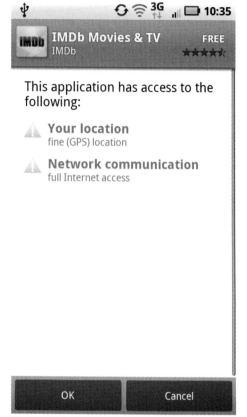

Figure 2.4
The services needed by the application

tion might use when it runs. Following that, however, is the additional step whereby you actually pay for the application (see Figure 2.6). Android uses the Google Checkout service, allowing you to pay for the application using either your mobile company (if the carrier supports it; currently, only T-Mobile does), meaning that the charge for the app will appear on your next bill or a credit card. If you elect to use a credit card, you will be prompted to enter the usual credit card information if it's not already in your Google Checkout account. When complete, your application will download and install. You also will receive a confirmation e-mail for your purchase.

## DOWNLOADING AND INSTALLING APPLICATIONS FROM OTHER SOURCES

Android is a completely open system, so developers are not required to use the official Android Market to distribute their applications. Instead, developers are free to distribute their applications directly from their own Web sites or via alternate markets. In order to download an alternate application, you need to find its location online. You can download the .APK file from the developer's site. If you are using your desktop or laptop computer, you need to transfer the application to your phone via USB, by e-mail or any other file-transfer method. You then can install the application. You also will need to specifically enable this ability on your phone by going into the phone's Settings from your Home screen and then selecting Applications and

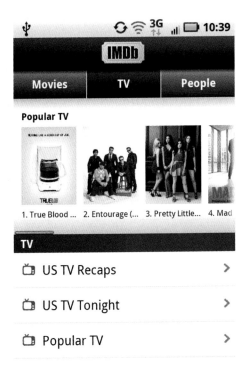

Figure 2.5
The application, ready to use

**TIDBIT**

AT&T locks down its Android-based devices, preventing their users from installing applications that do not come from the Market. However, a Windows-based application known as the Android Sideload Wonder Machine provides a legal, easy-to-use work-around. You can download the application and get details on using it at www.androidcentral.com/sideload-android-apps-all-you-want-sideload-wonder-machine.

as books and magazines, on buildings — anywhere, really. And they're not just for installing applications. They also can lead you to a Web page, video, or any other online content.

## KEEPING APPLICATIONS UP TO DATE

Android includes an automatic application update process by default. Whenever an application you have installed through the Android Market has an update available, the Notification Bar displays an icon letting you know that you have updates available. Expand the Notification Bar and select Updates available, which takes you to the My Downloads section of the Market. All apps that have current updates are displayed.

Select the app you want to update, read through the information screen, which often has information on what exactly has been updated in the app. If you want to run

enabling the check box labeled Unknown sources.

Many developers are providing an alternate and much easier way to install applications: QR codes, which look a lot like normal barcodes. You need to install the free Barcode Scanner app, available in the Android Market. Then when you encounter a barcode, you can scan the code using the phone's camera. The application displays the location of the app it found, at which point you can select the link to download the app. Note that barcodes may be found on Web sites or in printed materials such

## TIDBIT

Android 2.2 allows some applications to be installed on your device's SD card, rather than on the phone's internal memory. As the SD card provides expandable memory, this may allow you to install many more applications. Note, however, that this feature needs to be enabled by the application's developer, so it may not be possible on some, or even many, applications you download. Some widgets may not work if the application is installed on the card, and you may not be able to install if the card is mounted on your computer.

Figure 2.6
Purchasing the application

the update, select Update, which prompts you to be sure that you want to replace the older version of the app with the new one. After you select OK, you are taken to the screen that notifies you which services the app will use, and then the application downloads and installs.

Beginning with Android 2.2, you have the option to set an application to update itself automatically, in the background, without needing your permission (other than the initial OK). However, if an application's permissions (the services that are listed when it's initially installed) are changing, you'll have to update the application manually as a security measure.

## UNINSTALLING APPLICATIONS

Should you change your mind about keeping an application, you can unin-

stall it to free up additional space on your phone. Uninstalling an application involves going to the Downloads section of the Market and selecting the application. (Or, alternately, going to Settings>Applications>Manage applications) You are taken to the normal application page. Select Uninstall at the bottom of the page. You are asked to confirm whether you really want to uninstall (see Figure 2.7), and then are presented with a screen asking for the reason for the uninstall, which may help the developer improve the app for future customers (see

Figure 2.7
Uninstall confirmation

Please tell us why you removed this item:

◉ I don't use or want it.

◉ I need more space on my phone.

◉ It's defective.

◉ It's malicious.

◉ I'd rather not say.

Figure 2.8
Justifying your decision

Figure 2.8). Note that if you do not unin-stall a paid app within 24 hours of purchas-ing it, you will not be issued a refund when you uninstall.

# Your Home Screens

## The Skim

When I teach introductory Windows classes, one of the first things students always want to learn is how to customize their desktop. I have, in fact, been amazed by the number of students who take a two- or three-day class on something else entirely who nonetheless customize the desktop on the training center's computers. Your Android phone offers almost as much customization as your computer. As with your computer, you can change most of the appearance of the phone to make it more of an extension of your personality.

## ADDING APPLICATION SHORTCUTS TO YOUR HOME SCREEN

Once installed, all applications reside in the Applications Bin. Although you can search through the bin when you need an app, it will be easier if you add a shortcut to your home screen instead. You can add shortcuts by first opening the Applications Bin and finding the app you want. Then long-press the app until you feel the phone vibrate and the Application Bin collapses. Drop the app wherever you want on the home screen. You also can add shortcuts by long-pressing on your home screen and selecting Shortcuts. If you have an HTC Sense phone, you will find a plus icon on your home screen that you can tap to add shortcuts.

You can move apps around on the home screen by repeating the same procedure: long-press the app's shortcut until you feel the vibration and then drag it to a new location.

Remember that your device will actually have more than one home screen — usually, either five or seven. You can move shortcuts to other screens by dragging the shortcuts to the edge, waiting for the next screen to appear, and then dropping them in place.

You can remove shortcuts from the home screen by pressing and holding and dragging the shortcut to the Trash Can, which will be on the Applications Bin's tab. If you uninstall an application, its shortcut is removed automatically.

## ADDING WIDGETS TO YOUR HOME SCREEN

Many applications provide home screen widgets. A widget is essentially a miniature version of the application that runs directly from the home screen. Widgets can take up a lot of space on the home screen, or be the same size as an app shortcut. Either way, they provide instant access to the application's data.

You can add a widget to a home screen by long-pressing a blank area of the home screen until a menu appears that includes the option to add widgets. Select this option to bring up a list of all of the available applications that contain widgets (see Figure 3.1), and then select the desired application to add it to your home screen.

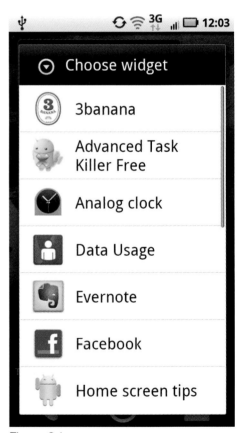

Figure 3.1
The applications I have that contain widgets

### TIDBIT

The Droid X and other devices running Motorola's version of Android include a set of Motorola widgets along with the Android widgets. Many of these widgets are actually quite useful. I'm particularly fond of the set of widgets that enable you to quickly toggle Wi-Fi, Bluetooth, GPS, and Airplane mode on and off; the Photo Slideshow is also pretty cool.

Widgets can be removed in the exact same manner as application shortcuts: long-press the widget and drag it to the Trash Can.

## ORGANIZE YOUR HOME SCREEN SHORTCUTS WITH FOLDERS

Folders enable you to organize your home screen, allowing you to place many more application shortcuts than might otherwise fit. You can create a folder by pressing and holding your finger on the home screen and then selecting Folders from the menu that appears. Another menu appears, asking you to determine which kind of folder you want (see Figure 3.2). Select New folder to create a new, blank folder on your home screen.

You can rename the folder by selecting the folder to open it and then pressing and holding again on the title bar of the folder. Applications can be added to the folder by dragging them onto its icon.

## CHANGING THE WALLPAPER

Just as you have likely customized the background or wallpaper on your computer, you can change the wallpaper on your device as well. To get started, long-press on the home screen and select Wallpapers. You then can choose Live Wallpapers, Media Gallery (to select a specific photo), or Wallpapers (to select a stock wallpaper). Alternately, you can press the menu key while on the home screen and select Wallpapers.

### Stock Wallpapers

Each device comes with a set of stock wallpaper art. My Droid X has 15 mostly

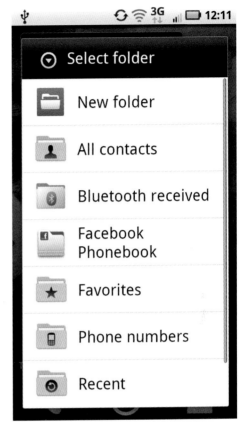

Figure 3.2
Types of folders on the Droid X

dark, moody, and abstract wallpaper designs, and my wife's LG Ally shipped with 33 wallpapers, most of them bright, happy landscapes. I suspect that these designs have as much to do with the target audience of the device as they do with any real design sense, although I am not sure what the Droid X's wallpapers say about me.

You can choose the wallpaper by selecting the Set wallpaper button. This selection returns you to your home screen, where you will see the new wallpaper stretched across all of your screens (see Figure 3.3).

Figure 3.3
The new wallpaper applied to the home screen

## Media Gallery

Your Media Gallery stores all of your images and videos. The gallery is discussed in detail in Chapter 9; for now, we will just use it to set the wallpaper using your own image. If you do not have any images in the gallery yet, you might skip ahead and read Chapter 9 now and then come back when you are done.

Using your own picture as the wallpaper involves selecting Media Gallery from the wallpaper options. The gallery opens, displaying all of the images currently stored on your SD card. Select the image you want to use and then crop it to the appropriate dimensions for the home screen. Select Save, and the picture is applied as the wallpaper.

## Live Wallpapers

Live wallpapers are essentially animated backgrounds for your home screen. As with the stock wallpapers, each device that supports live wallpapers ships with a slightly different set. Several of the live wallpapers display waveforms based on the currently playing music track. The Droid X includes a Google Maps live wallpaper that uses GPS to always display your current location. After you find the live wallpaper you want, click Set Wallpaper to apply it to the home screen (see Figure 3.4). You can download new live wallpapers from the Android Market. Note that older phones may not be able to run live wallpapers.

## USE OPEN HOME FOR FURTHER CUSTOMIZATION

You can take home screen customization even further by using one of the many applications that provide additional settings

### ALTERNATE APP

Many additional live wallpapers are available in the Android Market. Simply search for "live wallpaper" to view the list. A few are free, but most cost between $1 and $2.

Figure 3.4
Live wallpaper applied to the home screen

Figure 3.5
Open Home's default screen applied to the home screen

beyond adding and removing shortcuts and widgets and changing the wallpaper. One of the most popular of these is Open Home. Open Home is available for $4. After you install Open Home, you can purchase and install Open Home Themes, most of which cost around $1, although a few free ones exist. It seems that there is an Open Home theme for practically any hobby, interest, or obsession.

Open Home not only changes your desktop, it also customizes application and system icons. Figure 3.5 shows my Droid X

with Open Home installed. Although the wallpaper has not yet been changed, you can see that the App Launcher button and home screen navigation are all different. Also, all of the widgets and shortcuts I previously had placed on the home screen are gone.

# Actually Using Your Phone as a Phone

## The Skim

Recently, I was cleaning out the kitchen junk drawer when I stumbled across our old address book. Flipping through it made me chuckle, as it was littered with addresses that had been scribbled out and replaced as friends and family moved, and even entire entries that were crossed out for some now long-forgotten reason. Of course, it also was hopelessly disorganized; yes, the "a" names were under A, but they were in an essentially random order after that. The entire book was absolutely useless, because it was sitting, buried, in the back of the junk drawer as we had long since stopped using it, having transferred all of those addresses and phone numbers to the computer and, now, to our phones.

## ADDING CONTACTS

Your mobile device includes a powerful contact manager. Most people make most of their calls to a select group of people: friends, family, and co-workers. Although prior generations actually had to remember the phone numbers of the people they wanted to call, your phone now

41

can remember them for you, leaving you more memory for random Monty Python quotes and the like.

Because your Android device is synched with your Google account, you may find that you have contacts immediately upon setting up your phone, as any contacts you have in your Gmail account are imported. If you are using a mobile carrier that relies on SIM cards, such as T-Mobile or AT&T, your contacts from your previous phone likely also are imported.

Whether you begin with many contacts or have a completely empty Contacts list, you can begin adding new contacts right away, directly on your phone. Begin by opening the Contacts application, which can be found in the Applications Bin. You also can open Contacts by either selecting the Call button on the home screen or by pressing the Call button, if your phone has one.

After you are in your Contacts application, press your phone's Menu button

and select Add Contact or New Contact, depending on your model (see Figure 4.1). Enter any or all of the information for the contact. If you plan to use the contact for calls, then you will need to enter at least a name and a phone number. You can specify multiple numbers for each contact and set whether the number is for work, mobile, home, or any other custom type. If you have a picture of the person on your phone, you can also add the picture to the contacts, which will display both in the Contacts list and as caller ID when that person calls you or you call him.

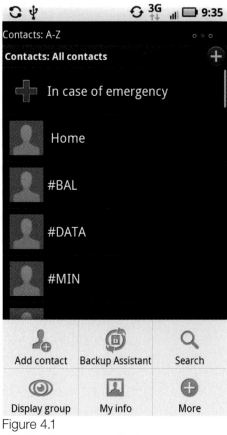

Figure 4.1
The Contact application's menu

**TIP**

If you want a particular contact to appear at the top of your Contacts list, add a space to the beginning of the name. In Figure 4.1, note that the first contact in my list is Home. It shows up there, rather than down with the other H contacts, because there is actually a space before the H, which causes the list to think that it should be alphabetized with the other contacts that start with nonalphabetic characters.

At the bottom of the Add Contact screen, select Additional Info or More to display more fields. The Droid X's Contact application enables you to enter birthday and anniversary dates, both of which are added to your calendar so that you do not forget them. Most Android devices provide fields for nicknames and Web sites for the person.

Each contact can have its own custom ringtone, so that you can tell who is calling without even looking at your phone. When adding the contact, select Ringtone and then select a ringtone from the list that appears. You also can use music you have uploaded to your phone as your contact's ringtone; see Chapter 8 for more information.

## TIP

If you have a contact for which you need to dial a number, wait a few seconds, and then dial an extension, you can add pauses into the number by entering commas between the number and the extension. Each comma adds a two-second pause. For example, if you needed to dial 555-1212, wait four seconds, and then dial extension 123, you could enter the number as 555-1212,,123.

## MANAGING CONTACTS ON YOUR COMPUTER

All of your device's contacts are automatically synchronized online via your Google account, meaning that you can manage contacts in either location. Sometimes, using your computer may be easier, particularly if your device has only a small on-screen keyboard.

Managing your contacts online involves going to www.gmail.com and logging in, using the same username and password you used when you initially set up the computer. After you log into Gmail, click Contacts on the left. You can click a contact in the list to bring up the details, which will match those on your phone.

## ORGANIZING CONTACTS INTO GROUPS

Scrolling through a long list of contacts every time you need to find someone can be time consuming. Android enables you to group your contacts into smaller lists so that they are more manageable. From your Contacts list, press the Menu button and then select Display Group. In the list that appears, select Create New Group. Enter a name for your group and select Add.

## ALTERNATE APP

Many alternate contact applications exist in the Market, but one of the nicer ones is aContacts. This Contact replacement displays your contacts in a picture-oriented interface, so if you have pictures associated with many of your contacts, you can pick that contact from a grid of pictures rather than a list of names. This app also enables you to set up multiple ways to contact people, including integration with social networking sites such as Facebook and Twitter.

**TIP**

If you use Outlook or another desktop e-mail program, you can very easily import your existing contacts into Gmail. You need to export the Contacts list from the program. The actual steps to do so will vary from one program to the next and even, in the case of Outlook at least, from one version to the next, but you should be able to find instructions online. Just make sure that you export the list in CSV format, or comma-separated values. Then from your Gmail contacts, click Import Contacts, select the exported file, and click Import. I recently went on a vacation with my family, and we discovered that we could not send postcards because several other family addresses were stuck at home in Outlook. Now that I have imported my Outlook contacts into Gmail, I never need to worry about that again.

Figure 4.2
Adding members to the group

Select the check box next to any contact you want to add to the group and then select Done (see Figure 4.2). Each contact can be added to as many groups as you want, so for example, a co-worker who is also a friend might be in both a Work group and a Friends group.

After you have your groups created, you can access them by either following the same first few steps: pressing the Menu button and then Display group. You can then select the name of the group to view its contacts. Alternately, you can select the list at the top of your Contacts list to see your groups.

You can also create and manage your groups in Gmail on your computer. When viewing your contacts, you will see a list of your groups on the left side of the page. Clicking any of these groups displays its members. When in a group, you can click the Add to Group button at the top of the page and type the name of a contact you want to add. When you are viewing the Detail page for a contact, you can click Groups at the top of the page to view a list of your available groups and check the box next to a group name to add the contact to it. On the main page of the contact list, the group to which a contact belongs is displayed on the far-right side of the page.

## CALLING A CONTACT

You can select any contact to display its details. From there, select the small green phone icon to place the call. You also can long-press a contact in the Contacts list and select Call Contact from the menu that appears.

If your phone has a dedicated Call button, you can press it to go directly into the dialer. If you do not have a Call button, you can select the phone icon from your home screen to place a call directly. In the dialer, you can select Contacts to view your list and then select the green phone icon to place the call (see Figure 4.3).

## MANUALLY DIALING NUMBERS

Although most of the calls you place likely will be to your contacts, of course, sometimes need to directly dial a number. Either press your phone's call button or select the phone icon on the home screen to launch the Dialer application. From there, select Dialer to display a normal phone keypad, type the number you want to call, and select the green phone icon to connect (see Figure 4.4).

Figure 4.3
Calling a contact from the dialer

### TIDBIT

Motorola includes additional home screen widgets on most of its phones. One of the more useful is the Contact quick tasks, which adds a widget personalized for a contact. The widget displays the contact's picture and can be customized to show up to four ways to connect to the contact, either via multiple phone numbers or multiple numbers to send text messages. After the contact is associated with the widget and the numbers entered, you can enable one-touch dialing so that you can select the widget and directly place a call. HTC Sense phones include a home screen widget that shows your favorite contacts.

45

Figure 4.4
Manually dialing a number

## USING FAVORITES

Those numbers that you call most frequently can be added to your Favorites list for easy access. You can call a Favorite directly by selecting the green phone icon.

To add a contact to your Favorites, long-press the contact's name on the Contacts list and then choose Add to Favorites. Likewise, if someone has fallen out of favor, you can long-press the contact on the Favorites list and select Remove from Favorites. While viewing a contact's details, you can select the small star icon to the right of the contact's name to add that contact to your favorites.

## SPEED DIAL

Not all Android devices support speed dial, instead relying on Favorites to provide quick access to frequently used contacts, but some devices such as the Droid X do have this long-standard feature. From the Dialer application, press the Menu button and select Speed dial setup. Next, select Add Speed dial and then select the contact. When set up, you can go to the dialer and long-press the appropriate speed dial number to connect. Honestly, although people have relied on speed dial to quickly reach contacts for years, in Android you probably can call a contact as quickly by going to your Favorites as you can by going to the Dialer, and using Favorites does not require that you memorize which contact is associated with which number, so this is not really all that exciting a feature. If you have a phone that does not support speed dialing, you are unlikely to miss it.

Whether or not your phone supports speed dial, all Android devices enable you to add a shortcut to your home screen to directly dial a number. To add one, long-press on the home screen, select Shortcuts, and then select Contact or Direct Dial.

## USING THE CALL LOG

Your phone's call log shows the most recent calls you have placed or received (see Figure 4.5). The number of calls listed in the log will vary from one device to the next. Although there are easier ways to connect to your contacts, the log is useful to return missed calls or call back to a number that you manually dialed.

An even more useful feature of the call log is the capability to add new contacts from it. If someone calls you, and you want

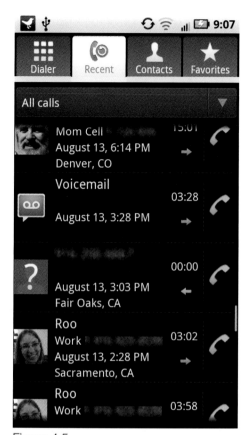

Figure 4.5
The call log

ing, it is unsafe to be distracted while you find a contact or manually dial a number, so voice dialing enables you to keep your eyes on the road and still place the call. From the Dialer application, go to the manual dialer and select the Voice Dial icon. Speak the name of the contact you want to call.

Of course, the steps required to get into the voice dialer pretty much defeat its purpose, so for added safety, you can add a shortcut to the home screen. The Droid X includes a Voice Commands application that enables you a considerable amount of control over your phone by talking to it. Although the application is discussed in detail in Chapter 14, you can use it now by launching the application and then saying "Call Home" or something similar (see Figure 4.6).

If your phone has a physical Call button, you have even easier access to the Voice Dialer: press and hold the Call button for about 4 seconds, and you should see the Voice Dialer appear.

to add him or her to your list, you can long-press the number and then select Add to contacts. From there, you have the option to either add the number to a new or an existing contact. If you select New, you are taken to the Add contact page, where the number will be filled in for you.

If you want to clear the log and remove the history of calls, you can press the Menu key and then select Clear list.

## VOICE DIALING

You can use voice dialing to place calls by talking to your phone. When you are driv-

### TIP

In order to effectively use voice dialing, you need to speak slowly and clearly. You also need to try to minimize background noise, so it may not be a terribly effective way to call someone from a crowded bar or rock concert. If you have a hands-free device, you can speak directly into its microphone, which is likely to be more effective than simply shouting in the general direction of the phone.

## CALLING FROM THE BROWSER

One of Android's nicest features is the way in which the phone functionality integrates with the Web browser. My wife and I recently have been trying to figure out how to get phone companies to stop sending us physical phone books, as we never use them anymore. Instead, when we need to call a local business, we use Google on our phones to look them up and then place the call directly from the Web.

Launch your phone's browser from your Applications Bin or, if you have one, a shortcut on the home screen. If you know the address of the Web site for the company or organization you are trying to reach, you can enter it directly; otherwise, search Google and then click the link to its site.

### TIP

You can do a local search on Google and likely get the company or organization's phone number without having to go to its site. In Google's search bar, type the name you want to search, followed by a city and state. For example, you could type "White House, Washington, DC." When the listing appears, you may see the number for the company directly on the Google results page, which you can click to go to the dialer. You can also search for people, although your results will vary. Be sure to spell their names correctly and include a city and state to increase your chances of finding them.

Figure 4.6
Using the Voice Commands application to place a call

When on the site, look around for their phone number; most sites have a Contact or About Us page that lists this, although many will place it on the bottom of each page. When you find the number, select it. This action opens the dialer with the number pre-entered, and you can press the Call button to place the call.

## USING THE SPEAKER PHONE

While placing a call, you can turn on the speaker phone so that you do not have to hold the phone up to your ear. To enable the speaker phone, select Speaker while the call is ringing or at any time during the call. Turn the speaker back off by pressing the same button. I find the speaker phone particularly useful when calling companies that are either entirely computer-driven, such as the monthly call I make to pay my mortgage electronically or when sitting on hold for an extended period of time. Note that the speaker is not an acceptable alternative to a hands-free device while driving, as you will need to hold the phone fairly close to your head in order to hear and be heard.

## CONFERENCE CALLING

You can speak to more than one person at a time using conference calling. To use this feature, place a call to the first person to whom you want to connect. Then while in that call, select Add Call. When the second call connects, select Merge calls to connect the second call to the first (see Figure 4.7).

## GOOGLE VOICE

Google Voice is the company's phone service. Google Voice gives you a dedicated phone number in an area code of your choosing. The Google Voice number is attached to you, not to any particular device, and can be set up to ring multiple phones simultaneously.

You can request a Google Voice number by visiting www.google.com/voice and logging in with your Google account username and password. You then are prompted to search for an available phone number by entering either a desired area code, city, or zip code or a word or phrase to which you want to map the number. You then can select from a list of available numbers. Next,

**TIDBIT**

The process outlined in this section on calling a number directly from the browser is, in fact, not limited to the browser. When you search for an address in the Google Maps application on your phone, you often will get the phone number at that address and will be able to select it to place the call directly within Maps. Many other applications provide similar functionality.

Figure 4.7
Merging calls

49

you need to enter a PIN to use for accessing your Google Voice voice mail and accept Google's terms and privacy policy. After you have your PIN selected, the system prompts you to enter a phone number to which you want to forward Google Voice calls. Finally, you are shown a screen with a two-digit confirmation key. Press the Call me now button to have Google Voice call you; when you answer, enter the two-digit number. At this point, your Google Voice account is set up.

After you have your Google Voice account set up, you can begin associating numbers such as your mobile device with it. That way, when someone calls your Google Voice number, the call is forwarded to your mobile.

## Installing the Google Voice App on Your Phone

To fully use the features of Google Voice on your phone, you need to install the free Google Voice application, which you can get from the Android Market. Once installed, the application enables you to associate your Google Voice account with your device.

The next step is to decide which calls you want to make with Google Voice. You have four options: use Google Voice to make all calls, do not use Google Voice to make any calls, only use Google Voice for international calls, and ask every time I make a call (see Figure 4.8). If you decide to use Google Voice to make calls, your Google Voice number appears as the caller ID for these calls, rather than your actual mobile number.

You also can use Google Voice as the voice mail provider for your phone, so that all calls are routed to the Google Voice Voicemail box instead of your regular voice mail. See the

Figure 4.8
Calling options with Google Voice

following section, "Google Voice Voicemail," for details on its advantages.

You also can enable a feature that sends you a text message whenever you get a call. Be aware that if you have a mobile plan with limited text messaging, you may not want to enable this feature.

## Google Voice Voicemail

When someone calls your Google Voice number and you do not answer, the call is transferred to your Google Voice Voicemail box. To your caller, the process is the same as any other voice mail. However, you have two options as to how to retrieve the voice mail message. You can call into Google Voice and listen to the message as normal, or you can read the message, thanks to Google Voice's transcription capabilities. Although the transcription is not always perfect, it will give you a good idea of what the message says. You can also view your voice mail box from any computer by logging into Google Voice in your browser.

## Placing Calls from Your Desktop Computer

As was shown in the section "Calling from the Browser," you can use your mobile device's browser to find a phone number on a Web site and call it directly. However, using Google Voice and the Mozilla Firefox browser, you can do the same from your desktop computer.

To enable this great feature, first you need to install Mozilla Firefox if you do not already have it by going to www.get-firefox.com. After you have the browser installed, go to https://addons.mozilla.org/en-US/firefox/addon/11167/ and click Add to Firefox. You may get a message stating that the extension has not been reviewed by Mozilla; if you do, click Add to Firefox again to continue. The extension should take no more than a few seconds to install, and you then are prompted to restart your browser.

After the browser restarts, you should see a message in the lower-right corner letting you know that the you need to enter your Google account information. Right-click on the message and select Settings. Type your Google username and password and click OK, and you see your Google Voice number displayed in the browser. Now, you can navigate to any page that contains a phone

Figure 4.9
Calling a number from the browser

number and click it. A message appears letting you know that Google Voice is calling the number (see Figure 4.9), and a few seconds later your mobile device will ring, saying you have a call from your Google Voice number. Accept the call, and it will ring through to the number you clicked on the browser.

## Other Google Voice Features

You can set personalized voice mail greetings for your contacts in Google Voice, so you can have one outgoing message for business contacts and another for friends and family. To set up this feature, open the contact in your computer's browser, either through the Google Voice page or your Gmail contacts and click Edit Google Voice Settings.

You can use Google Voice to place international calls, usually at much cheaper rates than you will find elsewhere. You need to add credits to your Google Voice account in order to pay for these calls, which can be done from the Google Voice home page on your computer. You can place the call from your browser, which then rings through to your phone, or if you have the Google Voice application installed on your phone and have configured it to either make all calls or all international calls, you can dial the number directly.

Google Voice also can be set up to receive text messages. Whenever you receive a text,

**TIP**

Many calling plans today include a feature that enables you to add a limited set of numbers from which calls are always free. A creative use of Google Voice can potentially enable you to get essentially unlimited calling minutes each month: add your Google Voice number to your free list and then give out your Google Voice number to your contacts rather than your actual mobile number. That way, almost all calls into your phone appear to be coming from the Google Voice number, and will, thus, be free.

of answering or sending the call to voice mail; if you choose the latter, you can listen as the message is left and press the star key to pick up. It is probably going to be fairly obvious that you were screening the call, though, so you might use this feature with caution.

Google Voice also enables you to send SMS, or text messages, via its service rather than your mobile providers. This essentially means that you can get around any charges your provider imposes for text messages you send.

it appears in the texting application in your phone, and also in your Google Voice inbox. In addition, you can configure the system to send you an e-mail when you receive a text.

The Block Caller feature of Google Voice enables you to permanently prevent particular callers from reaching you. From your Google Voice inbox on your computer, you can click the More link and then select Block Caller. When that caller attempts to contact you again, he or she gets a message that your number has been disconnected or is no longer in service. It is particularly handy for those annoying solicitation calls.

Back in ancient times, people used their answering machines to screen callers — they would let the call go through to the machine, listen to the message, and then pick up the phone if it turned out that the caller was someone to whom they actually wanted to speak. Voice mail systems long ago removed this capability, but for better or worse, Google Voice gives it back to you. When a call comes in, you have the option

# 21st-Century Communication

## The Skim

I spent the summer after graduating high school as an intern for my congressman. Not only was that my first experience in an office, it also was my first experience with e-mail. Later that year, after settling into the residence halls, I was lucky to be one of the first people in the hall to get Internet access in my room and, along with it, another e-mail account, although it relied on a system known as Kermit that was, even at the time, rather primitive.

Little did I know that I was not just learning some new toy, but rather learning something that would, decades later, become my primary means of communication. Most of my business contacts today are via e-mail, and, in fact, I have had exactly one phone conversation with the people at Wiley, the publishers of this book. Although publishing obviously happened before the advent of e-mail, I am not sure I would even know how to go about the publishing process without the connectivity offered by e-mail.

Within the last few months, I have had another major shift in the way I communicate. I still rely on e-mail, but today, my primary means of reading and writing e-mail has shifted from my laptop and desktop machines to my phone. Now, I only check messages on my computers when they include an attachment that I cannot open or edit on my phone.

# SWITCHING TO GMAIL

In 2004, Google began issuing invitations to a special beta of its newest service, Gmail, which it was touting as a new way to work with e-mail. I do not recall precisely when I got my then-coveted invite, but I do remember my initial first impression of Gmail; mostly, it seemed to be yet another free e-mail service. As I already had e-mail, both personal and business, coming into Outlook and already was using a separate Yahoo account to monitor groups, I did not really see the value of Gmail.

You stopped needing an invitation to join Gmail in 2007; in 2009, the company finally removed the "beta" label from the service. Over the years, I maintained my Gmail account as a repository for spam, but checked it only once every few months.

That all changed earlier this year, when, quite suddenly, my laptop died. I still do not know exactly what happened, but whatever fried the motherboard took the hard drive with it. Thankfully, all of my important documents, including the book I was writing at the time, were backed up on my home desktop computer, but I had been lax in backing up my Outlook file, so when the laptop died, I lost about six months of important e-mail. As I need access to e-mail when I'm away from home, switching over to Outlook on the desktop until I replaced the laptop was not really feasible, and the company with whom I host my Web site and, by extension, my personal e-mail provides an online e-mail application that is horrible, to put it nicely.

All of these factors, along with the fact that as an Android user I knew that I could easily get Gmail on my phone forced me to, at long last, take a serious look at Gmail, and it took only about a day to realize how horribly, completely wrong I had been all those years. Gmail is, in fact, far more than "just another free e-mail service."

## Signing Up with Gmail

If you do not already have a Gmail account, you can get one easily enough: simply go to www.gmail.com and click Create an Account. However, as an Android user, you almost certainly already have a Google account, so you, in fact, have a Gmail account as well, so rather than creating a new account, you should instead sign in with your username and password.

## Organizing E-mail

The most difficult thing about switching to Gmail from every other e-mail system I've used is getting used to Google's approach to e-mail organization. Outlook, along with every other desktop e-mail application, allows you to organize your e-mail into folders. Other free online e-mail systems such as Yahoo Mail follow the same model. In Gmail, however, you do not have folders. Really, all of your e-mail always simply resides in a mailbox. Instead, you use a concept known as labels to sort and filter your messages. The Inbox, in fact, is nothing more than one of those labels.

### Creating New Labels

To create new labels in your Gmail account, click Labels and then select Manage Labels from the buttons along the top of your inbox. On the Settings page that appears, type a new label and click Create. Should you create a label that you decide you do not want, you can click the remove the link next to the label in question.

## Manually Labeling Messages

You can apply a label to messages when they arrive in your inbox. Simply click the message to open it and then click the Labels drop-down and select the label you want to apply to the message (see Figure 5.1).

## Automatically Labeling Messages

When I used Outlook, I relied on its Rules feature to automatically move incoming messages into appropriate folders. With Gmail, I can use Filters to the same affect; incoming

## TIP

One of the advantages of using labels in Gmail as opposed to the traditional folder-based approach of other systems is that any message may have multiple labels applied to it. If you have a message that might logically fall under several different categories, you would have to either pick a single one or create duplicate copies of the message when using folders. With Gmail's Labels feature, you can apply all of the matching labels to a message, in effect organizing it into multiple categories.

Figure 5.1
Adding a label to a message

messages are automatically given appropriate labels. To create a filter, open a message that matches the criteria you want to use and then click the small drop-down arrow next to the Reply button and select Filter messages.

A page will now open, allowing you to set up the criteria you want to use for the filter. The e-mail address of the person who sent the message will be automatically set, but you can add criteria or remove the address and filter based on something else. When you have the criteria set, click Next Step.

The next page enables you to set the action to be taken by the filter. Although you can apply actions such as marking messages as read or deleting messages, I tend to use filters simply to apply labels. From the

drop-down list of labels, select the one you want to use; you also can choose New Label to create a label on the fly. When the label is selected, select the Also apply this filter to the conversations below check box and click Create Filter. From then on, messages matching the filter will have the appropriate label automatically applied when they arrive in your inbox.

## Viewing Messages by Label

On your main inbox page, you will see a list of your labels to the left (see Figure 5.2). You can click on any of these labels to view all of the messages tagged with that label (see Figure 5.3). In effect, this is the same functionality you had in your old e-mail

Figure 5.2

The list of labels on the Inbox page

system when you would view the messages in a folder, except with the important caveat that in Gmail, messages can have multiple labels, so a single message might appear under more than one label.

## Archiving Messages

A recent trend being pushed by organizational experts is known as inbox zero. The idea is that you want to keep your inbox empty by either deleting or filing all messages as soon as they arrive. Achieving inbox zero involves a fairly obvious procedure in folder-based e-mail systems: move each message you want to keep out of your inbox and into a folder. In Gmail, the solution is less obvious but in many ways easier. As

you have already seen, Gmail relies on labels to organize messages, but by default labeling a message does not remove it from the inbox view. Instead, you need to archive your messages. Archiving a message really does nothing more than remove the message from the inbox view. The message is not deleted. Instead, it will only show up when you view the messages for a particular label.

You can archive a message while reading it by simply clicking the Archive button at the top of the message's window. You can archive messages in bulk by clicking the check mark next to each message to be archived in the main inbox and then clicking the Archive button. Note that you can select a group of messages with different labels and archive

Figure 5.3
Messages under a particular label

them at once, something that you cannot do under traditional e-mail systems.

Note that archiving messages is useful even if you do not want to achieve inbox zero. One definite limitation of Gmail is that its Web-based interface limits the number of messages you can see at the same time, so if you have a lot of messages in your inbox, you may need to click the Next arrow button to see the next set. Archiving messages allows you to limit your inbox to only those very important messages you want to see at a glance. Note, however, the important difference between archiving and deleting. Archived messages remain in your mailbox, in the same way that a traditional e-mail program stores them in folders. Deleting messages removes them from the mailbox altogether, and deleted messages are removed permanently after 30 days.

## Searching Mail

Google is, of course, primarily a search company, so you would rightfully expect its e-mail system to include a powerful search capability, and you will not be disappointed when using Gmail. The top of every page in the system includes a search box that allows you to search either your own mail or the Web for particular terms. You can search for anything in the message, whether it is the sender's address or text in the body of the e-mail.

## Spam

Ever since Gary Thuerk sent the first unsolicited e-mail in 1978, spam has been an unfortunate fact of modern life. According to Wikipedia, 183 billion spam messages were being sent every day in January 2010, and that number is likely to continue to grow. All e-mail systems include some sort of spam filtering, but in all my years of being online and using e-mail, I have never worked with a system that filters messages as effectively as Gmail. In Outlook, I had my spam setting at its maximum, meaning that although almost no actual spam got through to my inbox, a lot of legitimate messages got marked as spam. This meant that I had to check my spam folder constantly for these false positives. The irony, of course, is that this meant that I was still needing to look at all of my spam.

Since switching to Gmail, I have gotten almost no spam. No e-mail system will ever be absolutely perfect in spam detection, so "almost no spam" is the best one can hope for. The real beauty of Gmail, though, is that I also have almost no false positives. I've gone from checking my spam folder several times a day to essentially never checking it at all. As I wrote this, I went ahead and looked in my spam folder just to verify that I was not lying. I currently have 852 spam messages there, and although I am not going to go through every one of them, I can say that none that have arrived in the last week are false positives. That is a far, far better percentage than I have seen on any other system, and yet another reason why I wonder why it took me so look to switch over to Gmail.

## Importing Your Other Accounts

An initial concern when switching to Gmail was my desire to keep my old e-mail account, which I have had for more than a decade. Fortunately, you can quite easily import almost any e-mail account to Gmail so that messages sent to it will appear in your inbox alongside any messages e-mailed to you directly at your gmail.com address.

To import other e-mail accounts, click the Settings link in the top-right corner of any page in Gmail and then select Accounts and Import. About halfway down this page, you will find a button labeled Add POP3 e-mail account. Click this button to launch the Import Wizard. You will need to provide the e-mail address you want to import, your username, password, and server for the account. If you do not know any of these details, you can ask your Internet service provider or your company's IT department for help.

## ACCESSING GMAIL ON YOUR PHONE

One of the biggest reasons to switch to Gmail as your primary source of e-mail is its close integration with Android phones. The Gmail application comes preinstalled on your phone, and, in fact, the process of configuring your phone and synching it to your Google account when you first purchased it completed the setup process for the e-mail. All you need to do is launch the program to start receiving e-mail (see Figure 5.4).

### Viewing Your Inbox

Gmail on your phone works almost exactly the same way as Gmail on your computer. As messages come in, you see an icon appear in your Notifications Bar. Slide the Notifications Bbar down to see details. If you have only a single unread message, the sender and first bit of the message will appear, but if you have more than one, you will see an indication of how many messages you have in that account. Select the notification to go to the Gmail application, which takes you directly to the first unread message. After reading, you can select one of the three buttons at the

**TIP**

Many larger corporations use Microsoft Exchange Server, which uses a system known as IMAP for sending e-mail, rather than the more common POP3. Gmail may be able to import messages from Exchange or other IMAP-based systems, but you will need to test it to be sure. Some organizations also may intentionally block third-party systems such as Gmail from accessing their servers, so it is possible that you will be unable to import your corporate mail. Thankfully, you may still be able to check your corporate e-mail on your phone, which will be discussed in "Getting Other E-mail on Your Phone," later in this chapter.

bottom to either archive or delete the message or go to the next oldest message in your inbox. You also can archive, label, or delete multiple messages at a time by selecting the check box next to the message and then selecting the appropriate option.

### Replying and Forwarding

If you want to reply to the message or forward it, you will see Reply, Reply to all, and Forward buttons, either at the top or bottom of the message, depending on the version of Gmail your device is running. Selecting either Reply or Reply to all will bring up a new message screen, enabling you to enter your response while displaying the original e-mail (see Figure 5.5). Selecting Forward likewise displays a new message, with the added necessary To field highlighted. In either case, your on-screen keyboard should

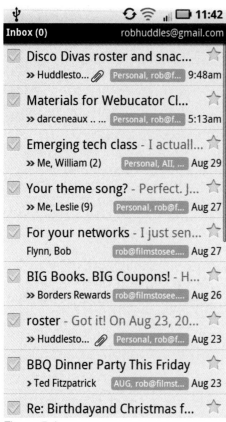

Figure 5.4
The preinstalled, preconfigured Gmail application

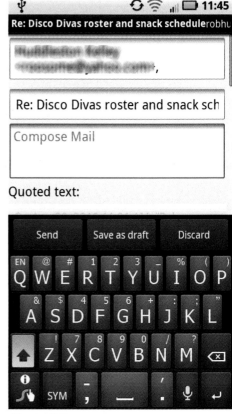

Figure 5.5
Replying to a message

appear automatically unless your device has a physical keyboard. When you finish entering your response or the forwarding address, select either Send to send the message immediately, Save as draft to continue working on it later, or Discard if you change your mind about sending it at all.

## Viewing HTML E-mail

Often, you receive messages that contain formatting and images. Your Gmail application automatically displays formatting in the message, but not images. This is done to

speed up the rendering of complex e-mails on slower connections, but at any time, you can select the Show pictures button at the top of the message to view images along with the e-mail.

## Viewing Messages by Label

As was discussed earlier, Gmail relies on labels rather than folders for organization. Any labels and filters you have set up on your computer are visible and accessible on your phone. From your main inbox, you can press the Menu key on your phone and then select View labels to see a list of all of the labels you have configured. Select a label to view the messages labeled with it (see Figure 5.6).

## Composing Mail

When you need to send a new message, click the Menu button on your phone and then select Compose from the options that appear. Enter the address of the person to whom you want to send the message, the subject, and the body and then select Send. You can also select Save as draft if you need to interrupt writing the message or Discard if you change your mind about sending the message.

Figure 5.6
Viewing messages for a particular label

## GETTING OTHER E-MAIL ON YOUR PHONE

While Gmail is probably the easiest e-mail system to use on your phone, you are by no means limited to it. (In fact, most phones don't even have the Gmail app on the main home screen by default.) In addition to the Gmail application, your phone comes preinstalled with another application, simply called Email. Using this application requires a few additional steps to set up. After launching the application, press the phone's Menu button, then select Manage accounts. On the next screen, select Add account, and then Email. Enter the e-mail address and your password for the account you want to use and select Next (see Figure 5.7). After that, one of two things will happen: either the account will be set up and

## ALTERNATE APP

Unlike its competitors, Android enables developers to create applications that directly compete with or supplant the built-in applications, and e-mail is no exception. One very popular alternate e-mail application is K-9, which offers improved controls over features such as how often messages are pulled from the server and the number of messages to display.

incoming and are mostly things that you will again need to verify with your IT staff.

After you complete the setup, you should see a message letting you know that the setup was successful and that you can now access your e-mail. Tap Done. You should then be taken to the e-mail application where you can view, reply, and manage your e-mail.

## INSTANT MESSAGING

Instant messaging has long been an effective way for people to keep in touch on their computers. IM, or chat, allows you to communicate in real time with one or more

ready to use, or, more likely, you will get a message saying that the account cannot be set up automatically and that you need to manually configure it.

When you need to manually configure the account, you are presented with four categories: General Settings, Incoming Server, Outgoing Server, and Other Settings. The General Settings screen will contain a name for the account, your name, and your e-mail account. The incoming server settings are one of the two places where you will likely need to make some configuration changes. At the top of the screen, set the type to the appropriate value; if you are using corporate e-mail, it likely needs to be changed from POP mail server to IMAP. Make sure that the server address is correct; contact your IT department if you are unsure what the server address is. The port is the really technical bit here; this is another setting you need to just check with your IT department. Double-check your username and password, and again ask IT whether you need a secure connection and certificate verification. The outgoing server settings are similar to the

Figure 5.7
Entering your username and password

others. Initially, chat systems suffered from a limitation whereby users could chat with other users only on the same system. If you wanted to chat with one friend who used only AOL's chat and another who relied on the MSN system, you would have to download and install two separate chat programs, one for each system. Today, many applications exist to allow you to chat on multiple systems at once, thus removing this limitation.

Thanks to several free applications available on Android, you can now take your chatting with you wherever you go. However, your phone also should have included the Google Talk application, which has the ability to connect to multiple accounts. To launch Talk, simply open your Application tray and select its icon.

When you first launch Talk, your Google contacts who also use the Google chat service will be displayed. You can see each contact's status, and begin chatting with any who currently are available by simply selecting his name (see Figure 5.8).

You can add connections by pressing your phone's Menu button and selecting Add friend. This selection opens a screen into which you can enter an e-mail address of the person with whom you want to chat and then send them an invitation. After your friend receives and approves the invitation, he will be added to your contact list.

## TEXTING

Texting was introduced fairly early in the development of mobile phones. Depending on your age, you likely either love or loathe texting, but even older users often can find it a useful means of communication — I receive at least as many texts from my dad as I do from anyone else. Of course, early

### TIP

When setting up your e-mail, you need to decide whether you want to delete the messages from the server or leave them. If you plan to rely on your phone as a secondary e-mail application, but still want to use Outlook or some other desktop application as your primary e-mail client, then make sure that you specify that your phone should not delete messages as it pulls them down. Be aware that the reverse also can cause issues: if you have your desktop client delete messages from the server as it retrieves them — which is a common and often default setting — then you will not be able to also get those messages on your phone.

### TIDBIT

Although your chat application will allow you to connect to multiple IM systems at the same time, you still need an account on each system in order to actually send or receive messages. Thankfully, all of these accounts are free, so while there will be some initial annoyance in connecting to a new friend who uses a system on which you are not yet registered, it should take only a few minutes to sign up. You also gain additional geek street cred when you belong to dozens of systems, so there's an advantage there as well.

## ALTERNATE APP

The application mentioned previously is one of many available chat systems. You might also want to look at Meebo, available in the Android Market. Meebo includes many features not available in Talk. Talk's biggest disadvantage is that you must send an invitation to anyone with whom you want to chat, even if you previously had connected with that person in another chat application. Meebo, on the other hand, connects directly to the various chat services, so you will have instant access to any friends lists that you already have established.

## TIP

Of course, you need to be careful when texting, as many mobile carriers impose significant costs on the practice. Most offer a plan with unlimited texting, but if you chose a different plan, you likely are limited on the number of texts you can send and receive before the bill starts going up. One friend of mine recently reported that her then-12-year-old daughter sent more than 18,000 text messages in a single month. Thankfully for both all involved, the family had an unlimited texting plan, as otherwise their phone bill likely would have been in the thousands of dollars.

Figure 5.8
Chatting with a contact

phones had a significant limitation on texting, as typing messages on a phone's dialer was annoying, to say the least. Typing the word "hello" on a traditional 10-key pad requires 13 keypresses: 44-33-555-555-666. Although some were able to learn to type longer messages quite quickly, most limited their messages or refused to adopt texting altogether because it was simply too difficult to type.

Your Android phone, of course, removes this limitation altogether, because whether it has a real keyboard or a virtual on-screen one, you have the full set of keys to work with, so typing "hello" is back to requiring only 5 keypresses. Even better, if your phone supports Swype, it is really one press-and-drag action.

## Sending Texts

Your phone should have a texting or SMS application built in. Sending a text is as easy as launching the application, selecting New text message, and then typing the name of the contact to whom you want to send the message. Watch your phone as you type, as it will offer suggestions of the contacts, so you should not need to type the entire name. You also can enter a phone number if you need to send a message to someone not in your contact list.

After entering the contact, tap in the message section to type your message. Be aware that the SMS system limits messages to 160 characters. Most phones these days allow you to send messages of any length, but longer messages likely are split. If you do not have an unlimited texting plan, this can result in a single message being counted as several against your plan or, if you are over your limit, result in multiple charges per message.

## Receiving Texts

When someone texts you, you will see an icon in your Notifications Bar and hear your default notification sound. Pull the Notifications Bar down to see who sent the message; select the message to read the full text. From there, you can type out a reply or press the Menu button and then delete to remove the message.

## SOCIAL NETWORKING

Social networking has become an important part in many people's lives. Whether

## TIDBIT

SMS stands for "Short Message Service." Although many think of texting as a relatively new phenomenon, it has been around for quite some time — it evolved from the radio telegraphy signals used in pagers, and the standards devices use to send and receive messages were adopted in 1985, although the first text message actually was sent on December 3, 1992. The idea of keeping messages short — the standard limits messages to 160 characters — was adopted because the original idea was to transmit the messages on otherwise-unused portions of the cell phone's signal. This allowed SMS to be supported instantly across the mobile space, so unlike modern technologies with 3G where available infrastructure often lags behind the user's desire to adopt, the SMS networks essentially already existed by the time anyone started using it. Today, texting is a massive industry, accounting by some estimates to close to $100 billion in revenue to carriers, in large part because although carriers charge customers to send and receive texts, the cost to the carrier for sending the messages is essentially zero.

you use it to reconnect to old friends or keep in touch with business associates, social networking allows even the most homebound to maintain relationships.

The two biggest social networks today are Facebook and Twitter, and your Android phone allows you to use both. Of course, you can use your phone's browser to view

## ALTERNATE APP

Although the default SMS application is serviceable, other alternatives do exist. Of particular note are chompSMS and Handcent SMS. chompSMS includes a fully customizable interface and the ability to create shortcuts for commonly texted words. Handcent SMS is likewise extremely customizable and has a Batch mode to send or delete multiple messages at once. Google Voice, which is discussed in detail in Chapter 4, can also serve as a text messaging application.

either of them via their Web interfaces, but a variety of applications on your phone make the process much easier.

## Facebook

As of June 2010, more than 300 million people were using Facebook, making it one of the five most-visited sites on the Web. From keeping up with the latest news from family members to playing social games, Facebook has become one of the primary motivators for many people to be online.

The Facebook application gives you many of the primary features of the site directly on your phone. Some Android devices ship with the application preinstalled, but if yours did not, you can find it, free-of-charge, in the Market.

When you first launch the application, you will be presented with a log-in screen. Enter your e-mail address and password — the same credentials you use to log into Facebook on the Web — to connect.

After you log in, you will be shown a Helpful tips page. Choose Finish to go to your News Feed and see the latest posts from your contacts (see Figure 5.9).

From any page in the application, either select the Facebook logo at the top of the screen or use your phone's Back button to access the application's main page. This main page displays links to the seven sections of the application, along with pictures recently posted by your contacts. Select Profile to view and edit your personal profile, write on your Wall, or access your Facebook photos.

Figure 5.9
The News Feed page

Returning to the main page, the Friends link displays your list of friends. You can select the link for any friend to be taken to his Profile page. The search box at the top of the screen allows you to quickly filter the list to find a particular friend. This is actually one of the features I like the most about the Android application, as Facebook's Web interface unfortunately makes it relatively cumbersome to get to this list.

The Photos link on the main page displays your Facebook photo gallery. The camera icon at the top of the screen launches your phone's camera application, enabling you to take and upload a picture directly to Facebook; see Chapter 9 for more details on using this feature.

The Events link displays your Facebook calendar. Although this is a feature of the Facebook Web site, I honestly never knew it was there until I used the Android application. In this case, the calendar is removing any excuses I might have had when forgetting someone's birthday.

From the main page, you can click Messages to view any messages that have been sent to you, view updates from Facebook, and see messages that you sent to your friends. Finally, the Requests page displays any friend requests you have pending. From here, you can either confirm or ignore the request.

If you want to update your status, you can select the icon at the top of the main page. This will take you back to the News Feed page and, if you have a virtual keyboard, open the keyboard to allow you to write your update.

### Facebook Widgets

The Facebook application allows you to install several widgets on your home screen.

## TIDBIT

To many users, the most important aspect of Facebook is the games, such as Farmville and Mafia Wars. The Facebook application does not yet directly support feeding your Farmville habit, although future versions might. However, many of the games, including Mafia Wars, can be played via your phone's browser. Simply go to the browser, navigate to Facebook.com, sign in, and play as usual. Other games such as Farmville, however, rely on Adobe Flash, and so you may or may not be able to play them on your phone. See Chapter 11 for details on whether or not your phone currently supports Flash Player.

## ALTERNATE APP

Another extremely popular Twitter client is the one created by Twitter itself: Twitter for Android. Like all clients, this one is free. Personally, I prefer the much-cleaner look and feel of Tweetdeck and the way it integrates messages from other social networks such as Facebook, but the official Twitter application is nonetheless a viable alternative. A close third place would be Twidroyd, which was the client I actually used before the release of Tweetdeck

## TIP

Twitter traditionally has had a very low adoption rate. Estimates are that less than one-third of those who sign up for the service actually use it regularly. Although I have had many friends and family members sign up, few have adopted Twitter and continue to use it. I almost joined that statistic: I did not start using the service heavily until about six months after I first joined. Part of the problem, I think, is that the design and layout of Twitter.com — most people's starting point — is truly horrible and a definite barrier to adoption. The other, I believe more important factor, is finding the right people to follow. That is what it did for me: For those first six months, I was following a bunch of people who were, frankly, not interesting to me. I did not get hooked on Twitter until I found several real-world friends who used it as an effective communication tool and then, through them, found many others to follow who were regularly posting updates that I found interesting. So, if the service does not grab you initially, give it time and try to find those key people to follow who will make it interesting to you.

These include a simple widget that displays the most recent post to your News Feed and allows you to quickly post your own updates, as well as a Facebook Phonebook folder that gives you a quick way to call any of your Facebook friends who have added their phone numbers to their Facebook profile. See Chapter 1 for details on adding widgets and folders to your home screen.

## Twitter

Twitter is a social network with an interesting twist: All messages or status updates on the system can be no more than 140 characters in length. Thus, it encourages, or some might say forces, its users to post only short, concise messages.

Dozens of applications exist to allow you to use Twitter on your Android device. My favorite is a fairly recent addition to the market: Tweetdeck, an adaptation of a popular desktop-based Twitter client.

You can sign up for Twitter for free by either visiting www.twitter.com on your browser in either your computer or your phone, or you can sign up for the service directly through Tweetdeck.

After you have an account, you need people to follow. Tweetdeck enables you to search for others on Twitter and then follow them. You can search by either Twitter username or, if the user included it in her profile, real name. For example, you can find me by either searching for my Twitter username, robhuddles, or by my real name. When you find someone you want to follow, simply select the Follow button on that person's profile page (see Figure 5.10), and you will begin receiving their "tweets" or updates in what is known as your timeline.

Thanks to the enforced brevity of tweets, you will be able to read the entirety of each message in your Timeline. Frequently, however, tweets will include pictures or links to Web sites. In this cases, you can choose the message to view it in its own window. If a picture is referenced in the tweet, you can view it. If it included a link, you can select the link to open the relevant page in your browser.

Social networks work only if they are a two-way street. Some of the people you fol-

Figure 5.10
Following someone on Twitter

low will decide to follow you back; others will find you by looking through the lists of people following those that they follow. You should contribute to the community by posting tweets that will be read by your followers. You can post these tweets by selecting the Update button at the bottom of the Tweetdeck window.

Type your post — remember that it must be no more than 140 characters — and select Send. The counter to the left of the button lets you know how many characters you have left. You will need to get used to the short character count, but after using the service for a while, you will get used to it.

### Replying to Tweets

If you want to reach out to someone you follow, you can target a message directly at him by beginning the post with the @ symbol and his username. For example, you can send me a message by posting to @rob-huddles. These tweets will appear in your target's timeline and be visible to anyone who follows both of you, but also will appear in a separate column in Tweetdeck. The columns are not readily visible as the application is optimized to fit on the small screen, but you can swipe the application window to the left to see your Replies column and view these posts. You also can reply to users you follow by selecting one of their posts in your timeline.

### Sending a Direct Message

You can send a message to another user, and only that user, by typing the letter d, followed by a space and her username. For example, you could direct message or DM me with d robhuddles. The difference between replies and direct messages is that any user who follows both you and the recipient will see replies, but only the recipient sees direct messages. However, in order to help prevent spam, Twitter imposes a special limit on direct messages: you can send only a DM to a user who you follow and who follows you back. Therefore, if you follow me and I follow you, we can DM one another, but if you are one of the million or so followers of a celebrity such as Adam Savage of the TV show *Mythbusters*, you cannot direct message him. By the way, Savage, who's Twitter username is @donttrythis, is well worth following.

### Retweeting

An important aspect of building the Twitter community is having users share information posted by other users, a process known as retweeting. You can take any message on your timeline and select it to view the details. Then select the Retweet button. You can edit the message and then select Send to post a copy of the original message to your timeline. The idea here is that while I might follow *Star Trek's* Wil Wheaton, you might not, so when he posts something I find interesting, I can retweet it. Now, even though you do not follow Wheaton, you will see what he posted through me. You can view the post and enjoy his wit or wisdom, and it might, and in the case of Wheaton should, encourage you to go ahead and start following him. Wheaton's Twitter name, by the way, is @wilw.

### Unfollowing Users

You might, for a variety of reasons, choose to stop following someone. Tweetdeck makes the process easy: simply select a tweet from a user, and then select his username. You will see a page that displays the profile of that user and includes an unfollow button: the button with the person and the small "x". Simply select this button to stop following. In case you are worried about offending someone, users are not informed when others stop following them.

### Facebook Integration

Tweetdeck integrates Facebook and other social networks into your timeline. Each network's items are displayed using a different color. You can add these networks by pressing the Menu button, then Accounts, and then selecting the plus sign next to each network (see Figure 5.11). Enter the account information for that network, and you will begin seeing its updates.

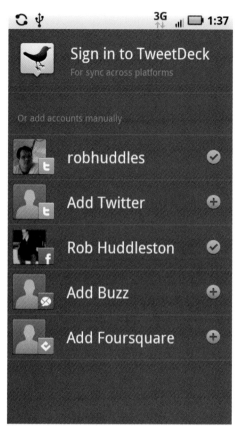

Figure 5.11
Adding social networks

# Managing Your Time

## The Skim

Google Calendar · To-Do List · Alarm Clock

When I quit my last full-time job and became an independent contractor, I knew that I needed an effective way to keep track of my schedule. Of particular importance was the ability to have a calendar that I could access anywhere, anytime. I also needed something that would be easy to use and require little or no setup. As I was just embarking on a new career and facing somewhat uncertain finances, whatever I ended up using needed to be free. Thankfully, I quite quickly found a solution that met all of those criteria: Google Calendar.

## GOOGLE CALENDAR

Google Calendar's Web-based interface ensured I could get to it easily, and as I began to explore its features I realized it offered even more advantages. Years later, Android's built-in integration with Google Calendar was a major selling point for me, as the phone would allow me to have true anywhere access to my schedule. As with other Google services, the calendar is free. You can access it online by simply going to www.google.com/calendar.

### Using the Google Calendar on Your Computer

Before you take a look at the calendar on your phone, I would like to spend some time showing you some of the key features of the calendar on your computer. This way, you can get an idea of how you can manage your time whether you are at your computer or on your phone.

### Viewing the Calendar

Your default calendar requires no setup: simply go to the calendar page when you are logged into Google and you will see it. Like other calendar applications, you have a variety of views to use to see your calendar. You can switch between these views using the buttons in the top-right corner of the screen (see Figure 6.1). You can view the calendar by day, by week, or by month. You also have an option of viewing four days at a time, which is a view very similar to the weekly but easier to work with on

smaller screens, and in a list-style Agenda view.

### Navigating the Calendar

The buttons in the top-left corner of the calendar allow you to navigate. In any view, you can use the arrow buttons to move back and forth; how far you move depends on the view, so the right arrow moves you ahead one day in the Day view, but one month in the Month view. At any point, you can click the Today button to return to, well, today.

To the left of the calendar itself, you see a monthly grid displayed at all times. You can click on any day to jump there, use the

Figure 6.1
Use the buttons in the top-right corner to change how you view the calendar. Shown here is the Month view.

arrows in this calendar to move forward or back through the months, or click directly on the name of the month to switch to Month view.

If you have a mouse with a scroll wheel, you can use it to navigate as well. While your mouse pointer is over the main calendar, scrolling up moves you backward in time, and scrolling down moves you forward, based on your view. You also can hover your mouse over the smaller monthly grid on the left and scroll quickly through the months.

### Add Events

You can add events to your calendar by simply clicking in the place where you need the event. If you are in the Day, Week, or 4 Days views, you can click in any half-hour space to add an event for that time; in the Month view, click on any day to automatically add an all-day event. The only exception here is the Agenda view, which does not allow you to add events by clicking in the window, although you can still add events using the other methods outlined later in this section.

When you add an event, you need to provide a name for the event. However, you often need to change other details of the event. For example, all events added in the Day, Month, and 4 Days views are assumed to be one-hour events, and all events added in the Month view are assumed to be all-day events. As the majority of things I need to track on the calendar are all-day events, I tend to stay in the Month view, but there are times when I need shorter events. If your schedule is better viewed in one of the other views, you likewise will encounter events that are more or less than one hour. You can change the timing and other details of

> **TIP**
>
> You quickly can alter the starting time for an event by including the time in the name if you use the Month view. For example, in the Month view, you can create a one-hour event by entering "Dinner with Editor 6pm". The calendar will add an event called Dinner with Editor, and set it as a one-hour event beginning at 6pm. This is a really great feature that saves me a lot of time when I need to add events that are not all-day. Unfortunately, it does not work on other views.

an event by clicking the Edit event details link. This will display the event in its own page, from which you can change the timing, along with adding details, such as the location and description of the event, configuring reminders, and changing how the calendar shows your time if you share the calendar with others.

You also can add events by clicking the Create Event button on the far-left side of the screen. This takes you directly to the event details page to add any and all information you need. The Quick Add link opens a small window into which you can type the name, time, and date of the event; the window includes an example of how to add an event. Both of these work in any view, including Agenda; in fact, they are the only ways to add events while in Agenda view.

You can edit an event's details at any time or delete the event by clicking on it in the calendar and then selecting the appropriate option.

### Adding Other Calendars

Before switching to Google Calendar, I was a longtime Outlook calendar user. In Outlook, I used to differentiate between business and personal events by color-coding, and it took me some time to figure out how to mimic this functionality in Google. As it turns out, you cannot directly color-code events; instead, you need to create individual calendars for each set of events you want to track. Although this seemed to require a lot of extra work when I first started using the calendar, I have discovered that it is, in fact, an extremely effective way to work. Separating events onto individual calendars allows you to quickly filter your calendar view to see only the events on that calendar. Also, you can share individual calendars with others, so, for example, I have several clients who have access to my work calendar so that they can know when I already am scheduled elsewhere, but they do not see my personal calendar. Likewise, I keep all school-related events for my kids on a separate calendar that I then can share easily with their grandparents.

You can add a new calendar by simply clicking the Add link in the My Calendars section on the left side of the screen. You need to give the calendar a name, but all of the other settings are optional. I have never exactly figured out where Google displays the description, so I never provide it. Users who work with people in other time zones likely will find the per-calendar time zone setting useful, while sharing the calendar will be discussed later.

Each calendar is automatically color-coded, which will determine the color of the bar indicating events on that calendar, but you can change the color by clicking on the small arrow to the right of the calendar's name after you get back to the main calendar screen. At any time, you can return to the calendar's settings page by clicking the same arrow and selecting Calendar settings.

Any event you add will be automatically added to your main or default calendar, but you can easily set an event to go onto a different calendar by choosing it in the drop-down list that will now appear when you add an event. You also can add an event to a calendar by clicking on the calendar's arrow in the left margin and selecting Create event on this calendar.

### Sharing Calendars

You can share your calendars with friends, family, co-workers, clients, and anyone else you might want. Each calendar can be configured individually; again, this is one of the biggest advantages of the Google system of separating events onto individual calendars. You can share a calendar by clicking the arrow button to the right of the calendar name in the left margin of the screen and selecting Calendar Settings. Then click the Share this calendar link.

You now have two options: You can make the calendar public, allowing anyone with the proper URL to access it, or you can share it with specific people. Many organizations rely on public calendars to share event information with members. As mentioned earlier, I rely on sharing my calendars with individuals such as my wife, my parents, and select clients.

When sharing with individuals, you can enter their e-mail addresses and then decide what permissions they have on the calendar. You can allow them to merely view the calendar, view your time as free or busy, make changes to events, or make changes and manage permissions for others.

### Adding Public Calendars

Google, along with many third parties, make public calendars available. Although you cannot edit these calendars, you can display their events in your calendar. You can add one of these calendars by clicking the Add button under the Other calendars section on the left side of the screen and selecting Browse Interesting Calendars. You can add holidays from just about any country in the world, add the schedule for your favorite sports team, or add birthdays from your contacts, moon phases, and more. After you find a calendar you like, simply click the Subscribe link.

### Adding Individual Calendars

If another Google user has shared a calendar with you, you can add it to your calendar. Click the same Add link you used earlier to access public calendars, but select Add a friend's calendar. You need to add the contact's e-mail address in the box that appears. If the calendar has been shared with you, it simply is added. If not, you are given the opportunity to send an e-mail asking the person to share his or her calendar.

## Using Google Calendar on Your Phone

Now that you understand how to use and manage the calendar on your computer, you can switch over and look at using it on your phone.

### Viewing the Calendar

Your phone will have shipped with a Calendar application, which will be available in your Applications bin. The calendar will open in the Day view, showing today and any events you might have scheduled for today (see Figure 6.2).

### Switching Views

You can switch to other views by pressing your phone's Menu button, which will display options to view the calendar in the Agenda, Week, and Month views. Ironically,

Figure 6.2
The default Day view on the Calendar

the designed-for-small-screens 4 Days view is not available on the very small mobile screens. The daily and weekly views display as many details of the events as they can in the space available, and the Month view simply displays bars representing events (see Figure 6.3). You can select any day on the Month view to switch back to Day view to see the details of the event.

## Adding Events on Your Phone

You can add events on your phone basically the same way you add them on the computer. In the Day and Month views,

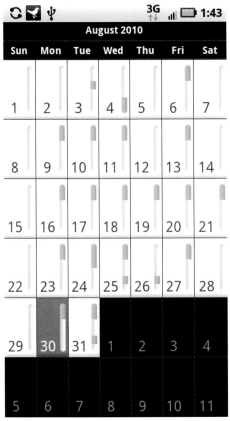

Figure 6.3
The Month view on the phone

long-press at the time you want to add the event and then select New event from the menu that appears. This displays the Create event screen that allows you to add all of the same information for the event that you would have on the computer.

## Viewing Calendars

Any events on any calendars you have set up on your computer will display on your phone. You can press the Menu button, then More, then View calendars to see a list of your calendars. From this screen, you can press Menu again to add another calendar, or uncheck calendars you don't want to see on your phone.

## Reminders

Events can have reminders associated with them to let you know when they are about to begin. When using the computer interface, reminders simply send an e-mail at the scheduled time before the event, but on your phone, they display in your Notification Bar and will play a sound — for me, at least, a much more effective reminder than simply receiving an e-mail. You can set the reminder when you create the event by pressing the phone's Menu button, selecting Add reminder, and then selecting the appropriate value in the pop-up menu. You can select the X button to the left of the Reminder pop-up to remove a reminder if you do not want it. You also can add a reminder to an event by pressing the Menu button while adding an event.

## Calendar Settings

You can access the calendar's settings by pressing the Menu button from any of the calendar's main views, and then selecting

More and then Settings. The primary settings revolve around how reminders should work, so you can set the ringtone to play and the default reminder time. You also have the option of setting whether the Week view displays all seven days or just Monday–Friday.

*Using a Calendar Home Screen Widget*

Some varieties of Android may include a home screen widget for the calendar (and can download some from the Market, too). The version that ships on the Droid X includes one that displays the current date and any events happening either today or tomorrow; I can select the widget to open the calendar's Day view (see Figure 6.4). Other varieties of Android may include a slightly different widget.

## TO-DO LIST

The Android operating system does not include a to-do list application by default. However, many to-do applications exist in the Market. One popular free application is Astrid.

When you first launch the application, you get an essentially blank screen with a text box at the bottom for you to begin entering tasks. After entering a task name, you can simply select the blue plus sign to the left of the text box to add the task.

You also can tap the icon to the right of the task name to open a truly impressive list of options for the task (see Figure 6.5). These options can be accessed for an already-existing task by long-pressing it in the task list and selecting Edit Task.

The Advanced tab of the settings enables you to configure task reminders, control its visibility, and set how often it should repeat.

The Add-ons tab enables you to add the task to your calendar and track your time while working on the task.

## ALARM CLOCK

I have never much cared to rely on the alarm clocks in hotel rooms, because I tend to have problems figuring out how to set them, and I am always afraid that the volume will either be too high or too low or that the radio alarm will be set to some station I would never want to wake up to. All of those concerns are a thing of the past thanks to the alarm clock provided in my

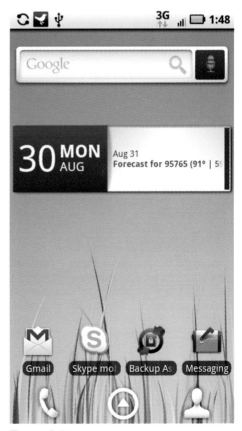

Figure 6.4
The Droid X Calendar widget

phone. The Alarm application is included as part of the Android system and is available in the Applications bin.

The alarm is incredibly simple to use: Select one of the alarms to access its settings. You can name the alarm if you want, or simply set its time. You also can configure exactly which ringtone or sound you want to use, and you can even configure the alarm to play one of the MP3s or videos on your phone. For those who are not inclined to wake up when the alarm goes off, there is even a backup alarm setting to play a loud beep if you ignore the main alarm.

When the alarm goes off, you can simply slide the bar to respond to it (see Figure 6.6). The settings screen enables you to configure whether sliding the bar dismisses the alarm or sets it to snooze so that it will remind you again in a few minutes.

A nice feature of the alarm is the ability to save as many alarms as you want. The application comes with three alarms set by default, but you can press the Menu button to add more, so if you have a series of important events to which you need

Figure 6.5
Basic task options, which show only a few of the many choices available to manage tasks

Figure 6.6
The alarm

reminders throughout the day, you can set them all at once.

The alarm clock also can serve as a timer. By selecting the Timer tab at the top of the screen, you can set the amount of time you want to count down from and choose Start (see Figure 6.7). The timer's settings, accessible via the Menu button, enable you to change the sound that should play when the timer goes off, set the phone to vibrate, and set a backup alarm.

Figure 6.7
Setting the timer

# PART II

# Maps, Music, Pictures, and the Web

# Maps

## The Skim

have to admit to being something of a map geek. For as long as I can remember, I have loved exploring maps. In college, my roommate and I had an awesome map of Antarctica on our wall; someday, I need to ask him what happened to it. I cannot bear to hear of someplace and not have any idea where it is.

The first generation of online maps did not foster my love of cartography. Those early maps were so painfully slow that they managed to suck whatever pleasure one might have gleaned from them; certainly, simply exploring the world was not a realistic option when each page could take 30 or more seconds to load. Today, however, not only can I waste hours randomly scrolling through maps online, I can do it on my phone. As a friend of mine likes to say, living in the future sure is cool.

## USING GOOGLE MAPS

Google Maps changed how many of us get directions in as big a way as Google Search changed the ways in which we find information online. Google certainly did not invent online maps, but it did figure out how to do it right, by providing an interface through which users

Figure 7.1

Maps, showing my location (blue arrow) by default

---

> ### TIP
>
> Watch your battery! Few things drain your phone's battery faster than GPS, so whenever you have Maps or any other application that uses it running, you are reducing your battery power dramatically. Merely locking your phone while Maps is up does not shut down the application nor turn off GPS, which is something I learned the hard way on my first Android phone. You need to avoid long-term use of GPS anytime you are not going to be able to plug in your phone either while you use it or shortly after.

could easily scroll around on the map and zoom in and out, and most important, it made sure that it would all be fast. Later, Google added services that made Maps even cooler, with things like satellite imagery and traffic reports.

Although finding directions from home works, being able to take those directions with you without having to waste paper is even better, and, of course, Google integrated its Maps application into Android from the very beginning.

You can open Maps from the Applications bin, but it is one of those applications that you are almost certainly going to want to add to your home screen as a shortcut. When you first open Maps, it should open to your current location, thanks to your phone's GPS system (see Figure 7.1).

When viewing a map, you can zoom in and out using the buttons in the lower-right corner of the screen. If you have a phone such as the Droid X that includes multi-

touch support, you can also zoom in and out by pinching the screen — place two fingers relatively far from each other and bring them closer while remaining in contact with the screen to zoom out, or use the opposite action to zoom in.

## SEARCH IN MAPS

Most of the time, when you use the Web-based interface for Google Maps, you begin by searching for an address. You can do the same in Maps on your phone — simply press the Menu button and select Search.

Type the address you want to find and select the magnifying glass button. You also can select the microphone button and speak your destination; this is a particularly useful, not to mention safe, feature for using Maps while driving. Assuming that the address you searched for was found, its location will now display on the map.

## GETTING DIRECTIONS

After you find a location on Maps, you can get directions to that location. When your search location appears, select the balloon tip that is displaying the address to see a screen with additional options for that location. Select the second icon along the top, and you will be given the choice between Navigate and Get directions. See the next section for details on Navigate; for now, select Get directions. Another screen then pops up with My location in the top box and the address you searched in the bottom. Slect Go to have the map generate driving directions.

Maps now displays a list of turn-by-turn directions to your location. You can select Show on map at the top of the screen to return to the Map view, where your route will be highlighted. Arrows at the bottom of the Map view enable you to step through the directions, while the small square icon in the bottom-left corner displays the directions list view again.

## GETTING THERE WITHOUT A CAR

If you would prefer to get where you need by foot, bicycle, or bus, Maps can help. When you look up an address and choose to get directions, you see four buttons along the top of the screen, just

> **TIP**
>
> Whether searching on your phone or on the Web, you do not need to know a specific address in order to find a location in Google Maps. You can search for an intersection by typing the names of the streets, so, for example, you could search for "Pennsylvania Ave and Executive Ave, Washington, DC" to find the corner near the White House. You also can search for local businesses near an address or landmark, so searching for "hotels near San Diego convention center" will give you ideas of where to stay for next year's Comic-Con. One of the coolest tips, though, will likely work only on your phone: searching "pizza near me" will show all of the pizza restaurants near your current location.

under the addresses. The first, a picture of a car, is the one that is selected by default and gives you driving directions. The second button with the bus picture gives you directions via public transit. The transit directions use any form of public transit available in your area, including bus, train, subway, and ferry. The directions show options based on your time of departure (see Figure 7.2), and the system creates a route that takes into account necessary transfers. A particularly nice feature is the included indicators for the fares each leg of the trip will require.

Bicycle and walking directions (with appropriate icons) take into account the differences afforded by those choices. Bike routes take into account special bike trails, and in big cities, they stick as much as possible to routes with dedicated bike lanes and avoid rider-unfriendly parts of the route like big hills. Walking directions ignore things like one-way roads and, similar to bike routes, keep you on as flat a route as possible and stick to walking trails if possible.

## THROW AWAY YOUR GPS DEVICE

In early 2010, Google rolled out a new, free application to many Android users, Navigate, which provides audio turn-by-

**Date & time**

**Departing 2:03pm**

**Trips**

| 2:10pm-2:28pm (17 min) | $2.00 |
| 10 | |

| 2:31pm-2:50pm (19 min) | $2.00 |
| 10 | |

| 2:51pm-3:10pm (19 min) | $2.00 |
| 10 | |

**Show later trips**

**Show earlier trips**

Figure 7.2
Getting there by bus

turn navigation to your destination. Given that I frequently travel to new cities, I had at times considered purchasing a dedicated GPS device, but I am very glad I waited. Why would I need a special device, along with its monthly subscription fees, when my phone does it for me?

Whenever you search for an address and then ask for directions in Maps, it will ask whether you want to use Maps (Get directions) or Navigate. Navigate generally takes a few seconds to load, but after it does, you will see your route highlighted on the screen. The orientation switches to that roughly first-person perspective you probably have seen in dedicated GPS navigation systems (see Figure 7.3). You then receive turn-by-turn directions as you drive, using Navigate's built-in text-to-speech voice, which my daughter decided was named Sierra.

When you reach your destination, you should turn Navigate off. If it keeps running, even in the background, it will drain your battery very quickly. Press the Menu button on your phone and choose Exit Navigate to close it and save battery life.

By the way, I was kidding in the heading about throwing away your GPS device. Like all modern electronics, it has all kinds of nasty chemicals in it, so be sure to recycle it instead!

## VIEW LIVE TRAFFIC

Maps will show you live traffic reports, allowing you to route yourself around problem areas. You can turn this feature on by pressing the Menu button on your phone and then selecting Layers. Select Traffic, and the map updates to display traffic reports. Green lines on roads mean that everything is fine; yellow lines mean you should expect

Figure 7.3
Turn-by-turn directions, thanks to Navigate

traffic to be slow but still moving, and red roads are the ones you want to avoid (see Figure 7.4). Road hazards are displayed as well: An orange triangle icon signifies construction, while an icon of a collision signifies some other hazard, such as an accident or disabled vehicle.

## OTHER LAYERS

The Layers feature in Google Maps allows you to see the world in a variety of different ways. Traffic is a layer, but others exist as well. Each of these layers can be accessed by pressing your phone's Menu button, and then selecting Layers.

## Satellite Photos

Instead of the traditional drawn map, you can view your route using satellite images. Personally, I tend to prefer the map view when I need to travel, but I have found the satellite view useful on occasion when trying to find a location: Seeing what the area around my destination actually looks like can be very helpful when I get close.

Figure 7.4
Monday afternoon traffic in New York City — Yuck!

## Terrain Maps

Another layer available on Google Maps is Terrain. Hikers would find this particularly useful in planning routes.

## Buzz

Google Buzz integrates social networking with Google Maps and the company's other services such as Mail. With Buzz, you post status updates, similar to Facebook or Twitter. Each user's updates then appear on the map as a small thought bubble icon. You can select the icon to read the status, or select

the colorful icon in the bottom-right corner of the map to post your own.

## Latitude

Google Latitude enables you to share your location with others and easily connect when nearby. When you select the Latitude layer, it displays your current location. You can select your name to display a list of options, including Send location to others. You have the option to broadcast this location on Facebook, Twitter, or other social networks, as well as text or e-mail it. If you join Latitude through its dedicated app, you also can send and receive invitations from friends and then easily discover their location. More information on Latitude is available at www.google.com/mobile/latitude.

## Recent Places

The final set of options on the Layers menu lists the locations you have most recently searched, making it easy to look up a recent location and display it on the map.

## More Layers

Select the More Layers button at the bottom of the Layers menu screen to see additional choices. The My Maps option displays maps you have created and saved on the Google Maps Web page. More details on creating and saving maps can be found at http://maps.google.com/support/bin/static.py?hl=en&page=guide. cs&guide=21670&topic=21676. The Bicycling layer displays local bike paths and routes (see Figure 7.5), and Wikipedia overlays icons on the map that link to Wikipedia entries for your area. The Transit Lines layer displays bus, train, and subway maps (see Figure 7.6). Finally, Favorite

Figure 7.5
Bike paths in Sacramento, California

Figure 7.6
New York City's transit map

Places enables you to view maps created by other users.

## DRIVING WITH YOUR PHONE

Features like Navigate are obviously most useful when used in your car. They are less useful, however, if your phone is simply sitting on the center console or in your pocket; in order to really benefit from the turn-by-turn directions, you need to be able to see your phone. You can maximize both the safety and convenience of these features by purchasing a car dock, which is a device

designed to securely hold your phone on your dashboard. Each model of phone has a car dock specifically designed for it, so be sure to get the right one. Most car docks include a car charger, so if you are planning on getting a dock, you may not need to spend the additional money on a separate charger.

Many newer Android phones include a CarDock application that puts the phone into a state ready to use in your car. The phone automatically should detect when it has been put in the dock and switch to car mode by itself; if it does not, you can launch

93

## TIDBIT

GPS stands for Global Position-ing System. Although consumer-level GPS is relatively new, the technology has been around for a while. The U.S. government began work on it in 1973, with the system becoming fully operational by 1995. The system relies on between 24 and 32 satellites and is still funded by the U.S. government and run by the U.S. Air Force. The system was designed to allow the Air Force and Navy to more precisely locate and control military assets, but following the 1983 destruction of Korean Air Lines flight 007, which was shot down after straying accidentally into restricted Soviet airspace, the U.S. government opened the system to civilian use as well. Today's GPS is capable of providing a location anywhere on the planet to within 20 meters, or about 65 feet.

the application manually. On the Droid X, the application includes six oversized, easy-to-hit buttons. Five are preprogrammed for music, maps, calling, voice search, and closing the application. The sixth is custom-izable and can be linked to any other appli-cation on your phone. When I first began playing with CarDock, I set this sixth button to the camera, which seemed kind of fun. When I was done playing, though, I reset it to launch the application I use the most in the car: StreamFurious, which allows me to listen to Internet radio stations.

Whenever I drive, I keep the phone in the dock. I usually launch StreamFurious and set it to the station I want to listen to, and then select the My Location button in Car-

Dock. This ties directly into Google Maps, so if you have a layer already turned on, it will display; I almost always leave Traffic on. CarDock includes a few additional features, such as a speed and direction indicator in the bottom-left corner of the map. You can also search for a location and turn on Navi-gate to have your docked phone look and act just like a dedicated GPS device.

When you receive a call while the phone is docked, it will interrupt whatever else the application may be doing to display the incoming call. If you have a Bluetooth headset or other hands-free device, you can accept the call by simply selecting the appropriate button. If you do not have a hands-free device, you can still accept the call, at which point CarDock will turn on the speaker phone, in theory allowing you to have your conversation without needing to hold the phone to your ear. I say "theoreti-cally" because although it does work, you will find that the noise in your car will likely be too loud to really talk on the phone this way.

A particularly nice feature of the dock is the integrated jack on the back that allows you to plug your phone in, because many features — particularly Navigate — would otherwise quickly drain the battery. Be aware, however, that your phone is likely sitting exposed on your dashboard and is liable to overheating, something that has happened to me on several occasions when it has been more than 100 degrees outside. When the phone begins to overheat, the first thing it will do is stop charging, so you should glance at the Notification Bar every now and then and note whether you are still charging. If it occurs, remove the phone from the dock and move it someplace out of the sun until it can cool down. It is also possible that given that you are using the screen, GPS, Navigate, and other applications, the car charger will not be able to actually charge the phone, but will instead just keep it from discharging. Thus, you may find that when you arrive at your destination, your battery will not be at 100 percent.

Many newer cars include an input jack to allow you to plug a device into the car stereo. Because your phone uses a standard jack for the headphone, you can plug your phone in and listen to music, Internet radio, or Navigate's directions over the car's speakers.

## STREET VIEW

Street view is perhaps one of Google's best-known features of Maps, so it is fairly surprising that although it is available on your phone, it is very well hidden. Street view allows you to see photographs of an area on the map, complete with 360-degree views. If you need to find a business or something in an unfamiliar location, this can allow you to see the area to which you are traveling. Note that like satellite photos, Street view is not live.

To access Street view, you need to zoom in on the map. As you get close to the ground, you begin to see buildings rendered in 3-D. At this point, you can long-press on a point on the map, which displays an address. Select the address to bring up a screen with details of that address, and you should see an icon on the far right of a person with an arrow. If the icon is grayed out, you have not zoomed in far enough to use Street view.

If you have zoomed in enough, the icon will be active, and selecting it will display that location in Street view (see Figure 7.7).

Figure 7.7
Google Headquarters in Mountain View, California, as seen on Street view

You can swipe your finger to turn the view around and see around you, or use the dark arrows to move forward or backward.

## GOOGLE PLACES

Recent versions of Google Maps include a new feature called Google Places, which displays information on restaurants, coffee shops, bars, hotels, attractions, ATMs, and gas stations near your current location. Places can be accessed by selecting the pushpin icon at the top of the Google Maps screen. Selecting this icon displays a menu

95

of categories; selecting a category from this menu displays businesses matching that category. You then can select any of these locations to bring up more details about a business, get directions to it, or call the business directly.

## INSTALL A COMPASS

Your phone includes an internal compass that, among other things, ensures that the Navigate arrow is pointing in the right direction. The Android Market includes a Compass application that displays this directional awareness as a traditional compass (see Figure 7.8).

When you first launch the compass, it will prompt you to calibrate it by waving the phone in a figure-8 pattern several times. You might want to do this when no one else is around because you will look rather silly doing it.

You can press the Menu button to change the settings of the compass, including changing the type to look like an antique compass or a GPS device that includes your speed, pitch, and roll.

Figure 7.8
The Compass application

## FIND OUT WHERE YOU WERE WITH MY TRACKS

The My Tracks application, available in the Market, enables you to track your location while walking, hiking, or other activities. These recorded paths then can be uploaded and saved and shared either as custom Google Maps or Google Docs. You can also view live statistics of your path while you go.

The first time you launch My Tracks, you need to agree to the license agreement and then, if you want, read the provided help file. After that, you are taken to a map that displays your current location. You can press the Menu button on your phone and select Record Track to begin recording. Then simply walk, run, hike, or drive the path you want to take. While on your route, you can select the map and then select the right arrow button that appears to view a screen of statistics about your track, or the left arrow to view an elevation profile.

When you have completed your path or route, you can again press the Menu button and then select Stop Recording, which displays a Track Details page, where you can give the track a name, input the type of activity, and describe the track. When complete, select Save.

To share the track, select the plus icon in the bottom-right corner of the screen and select the option you want to use. The Send to Google option uploads the map to either Google Maps or Google Docs, and Share with Friends enables you to e-mail a link to the map or send the track in one of several file formats.

## USE GOOGLE EARTH

Few applications have brought out the map geek in me more than Google Earth. Earth is an amazing application that combines Google's database of satellite imagery together in a single, easy-to-explore interface. Earth was developed by another company, Keyhole, and released under its current Google Earth name in 2005. It now can be downloaded for free from the Android Market, bringing all of its coolness to your phone.

When you first launch Google Earth, you can pretend momentarily that you are an astronaut, as you will see Earth from a distance that so far has only been viewed by the Apollo astronauts.

You can rotate the globe by simply sliding your finger over it, and zoom in by either moving two fingers apart from one another on the screen or by double-tapping. Eventually, details begin to appear. When you are in far enough to make out details, you will see yellow squares marking designated locations; selecting any of these will bring up a screen detailing that location. You can press your phone's Back button to return to the main Google Earth screen from these detail pages.

Normally, dragging your finger on the screen moves you around the map. You can select the Look Around icon in the

### TIDBIT

Unfortunately, the list of Android devices that support Earth is far shorter than the list of ones that do. According to the Google Earth Web site at http://earth.google.com/support/bin/answer.py?hl=en&answer=174898, only the Nexus One and Droids that run at least Android 2.1 support it. If you are unsure whether your phone supports this app, simply search for Google Earth in the Market — if it shows up, then you are in luck; if not, then sorry. That is bad news for most Android users, but of course, the good news is that Android-based devices are only going to get better as time goes on, and so is your phone.

bottom-left corner of the screen to change this behavior. With Look Around enabled, dragging your finger will rotate your view 360 degrees around the center of the screen. You can select the icon again to turn off Look Around, and select the compass in the top right-corner of the screen to return to a north-is-up orientation.

With Look Around turned on, you can tilt your view so that rather than looking from above, you can see the world from more of an angle. You can tilt down by dragging upward on the screen (see Figure 7.9), or tilt up by dragging down on the screen. Although the directions may seem backward — you drag up to tilt down, and drag down to tilt up — they actually make a lot of sense when you are interacting with the application.

No Google application would be complete without Search, and Google Earth is no different. Press the Menu button on your phone and select Search, or press your phone's Search button. Then type what you are looking for, whether it is an address, landmark, business, or just about anything else. For the most part, the same searches that work on Google Maps work here. The main difference is the cool factor: in Maps, you are simply taken to your destination, while in Earth, you get to fly there. When the original Google Earth application was released, one reviewer described the animation as an "ICBM view," which is apt as it will look like you take off, fly over the planet, and then dive in on your location (see Figure 7.10).

Unfortunately, many of the desktop application's really neat features are missing in this first version of the Android application, including the ability to go back in time and see older satellite photos of regions (using this ability to see pictures of New Orleans before and after Katrina is particularly moving) and exploring the Moon and Mars. Hopefully, Google will add them as time goes by.

Figure 7.10
"ICBM view" of Google Earth

Figure 7.9
Seeing Sacramento at an angle

# Music

## The Skim

M y entire music collection exists today as MP3s. We have a really cool CD rack we bought from Ikea on the wall of our living room, but honestly it exists mostly for decoration. On the rare occasion that I still purchase a CD, I bring it home and immediately rip it or convert it to MP3s on the computer. The CD itself finds its way to the Ikea case, never to be seen or heard again. I know I am not alone here, either; I cannot think of anyone I know who still uses actual CDs as their primary source for music, and why would they? Why would I want to listen to a single album, and have to keep interrupting myself to change albums, when I can create a playlist of all of the songs I want to listen to and just let it play? This is even more true when you consider that today, you can bring your music collection with you anywhere you go. Best of all, you do not need to buy and carry around a separate MP3 player, either.

## PREPARING MUSIC FOR YOUR PHONE

In order to transfer music from a CD to your phone, you first need to convert it to the correct format. Dozens of programs exist that are capable of performing this task, but the most popular is Apple's iTunes application. If you own a Mac, you already have iTunes installed; if you use Windows, you can download it free from www.apple.com.

## Ripping CDs

You can transfer the music from a CD to your computer's hard drive via a process known as ripping the CD. To do this, simply insert the CD into your computer's drive with iTunes running. The program will detect the CD and ask whether you want to import it into your iTunes library (see Figure 8.1). Click Yes, and the program begins ripping the songs from the CD.

When the ripping process is complete, you can click Music from the Library menu

on the left side of the screen to see the songs that have been downloaded (see Figure 8.2). Unlike many programs, iTunes does not directly display the location of the music on your hard drive, as it assumes that you will use the program to perform all tasks on the songs. However, if you are curious as to where exactly the music is stored, you can right-click on a track and select Get Info. The file's location is displayed at the bottom of the dialog box.

## Change iTunes Settings

iTunes automatically converts your tracks to M4A format. This format should be fully supported by your Android device and practically any other media player you want to

**Figure 8.1**
iTunes asking whether I want to import a CD onto my machine

Figure 8.2
The CD's tracks, now transferred to my computer, displaying in the iTunes library

use, but if you need or want to use the more common MP3 format, you can change the settings in iTunes to accommodate that. Click Edit and then Preferences. On the first tab of the Preferences dialog box, select Import Settings. In the Import Settings dialog box, change the Import Using drop-down from the default AAC Encoder to MP3 Encoder. The Preferences dialog box also can be used to change the default location to which iTunes copies music files by clicking the Advanced tab, and then Change.

## Download Album Art

iTunes can download album art for your albums, which displays both in the iTunes library when you listen to the album on your computer as well as on your phone. In order to download album art, however, you first need to create an account with iTunes and log into the iTunes store. You can do this directly within iTunes by clicking the iTunes Store link on the menu at the left. Then click Sign In in the top-right corner. If you already have an account, you can enter your username and password; if you do not have an account yet, click Create New Account (see Figure 8.3).

After you are logged in, you can return to your music library. Then right-click the album and select Get Album Artwork. You need to confirm that, yes, you really did want to download the artwork — I would suggest that you select the Do not ask me

## TIP

No discussion of working with music files would be complete without a discussion of copyright issues. When you purchase an audio CD, you have the legal right to copy that music to another medium such as your computer so long as you are going to use that music only for you to listen to. You cannot distribute the music files to others or use it for any public performance. You can find many more details on this and other issue surrounding copyright from the U.S. Copyright Office's Web site at www.copyright.gov/.

again option on this useless dialog box — and the album art will appear.

## DOWNLOADING MUSIC TO YOUR PHONE

iTunes does not support directly synching songs between itself and non-Apple devices, but you can still transfer music between your computer and phone manually. Although some other media players on your computer may support directly transferring songs, the steps outlined in this chapter work regardless of the software you use.

To transfer your music, you first need to plug your phone into your computer's USB port and mount your SD card. You can mount your card by pulling down the

Figure 8.3
Log into iTunes using an existing account or create a new one.

Notification Bar and selecting USB connection. Then depending on your version of Android, select either Mount card or PC Mode or USB Mass Storage. See Chapter 1 for a discussion on the differences between PC Mode and USB Mass Storage.

When mounted, your phone's SD card should appear as a drive on your computer. From here, you can drag-and-drop music files from whatever folder iTunes stored them in to the Music folder on your phone.

## PURCHASING MUSIC VIA AMAZON MP3

In addition to copying music from your computer to your phone, you also can purchase music directly on your phone. Although many applications exist to do this, most Android phones come with a preinstalled application to enable you to purchase music from Amazon. You can launch the Amazon MP3 app from your Application Launcher. From here, you can either search for a song or album or browse bestselling albums, songs, or genres (see Figure 8.4). When you find what you are looking for, you can select the album to display the tracks. From here, you can either purchase the entire album or individual songs by selecting the price and then selecting it again when it turns into a Buy button.

Next, you are prompted to log into your Amazon.com account; you can click the link at the top of the dialog box to create one if necessary. As soon as you log in, the purchase process begins automatically and cannot be cancelled, so be sure you want to purchase the album before entering your username and password.

Note that the Amazon MP3 store is not available in some countries, so it is possible

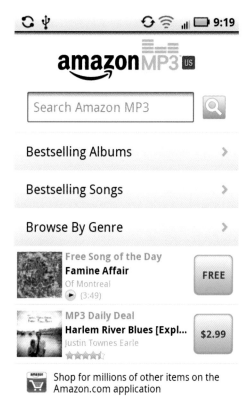

Figure 8.4
Amazon MP3's starting page

that your phone will not support it, depending on your location.

## LISTENING TO MUSIC

After you have your music on your phone, you can use Android's built-in music player to listen to it. Simply launch the Music app from your Application Launcher to see a list of the albums on your phone (see Figure 8.5). Choose an album to see a list of the tracks, and select any song to begin playing.

While a song is playing, you can pause it or move to the previous or next song using the buttons at the bottom of the screen. You

**TIP**

The Music app underwent an important, and in my eyes, negative change sometime between Android 1.6 and 2.1. When I would listen to songs on my G1 running 1.6, the album list displayed songs in track order, so if I selected the first song in the album, it would play through all of the songs in the order the artist intended. In Android 2.1, however, the tracks are listed alphabetically. This is fine if the track's filename happens to begin with the track number, but if the track does not, you get the songs in a rather arbitrary order. Fortunately, there is a workaround: From the album list, you can long-press the album and select Play from the menu that appears, which plays the album in track order. We can hope that Google will fix, or rather refix, this in some future release.

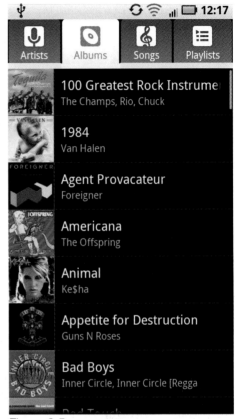

Figure 8.5
The album list in the Music app

also can drag the slider to move backward or forward through a song or press and hold your finger on the Forward or Back buttons to fast-forward or fast-reverse the current song. Higher on the screen, just below the album art, are three buttons that enable you to return to the track list, shuffle the songs to play the album in a random order, or repeat the current song. You also can select the album art itself to switch between the art and an animated visualization while the song plays. You can use your phone's Back button to return to the track list and then use the button again to return to the album list. From here, you can view your music by artist or song. You can also select the Playlists tab to display any playlists you may have

on your phone; see "Creating Playlists" later in this chapter.

You can use any other function of your phone while a song is playing. Simply press the Home button to return to the home screen. The Notification Bar displays an icon letting you know that a song is playing; you can pull the Notification Bar down to view the title, album, and artist of the song. Select the notification to return to the Now Playing screen.

Your music also continues playing when the phone sleeps. On some versions of Android, the Lock screen displays the current song and provides buttons that enable you to pause, skip forward, and skip back without unlocking your phone (see Figure 8.6).

## CREATING PLAYLISTS

Often, you want to play songs from more than one album. You might have a mix of songs you happen to like, or perhaps have a series of albums you listen to in succession. Either of these can be handled easily with a playlist. You can create playlists from songs currently on your phone. To

do this, long-press a song — either directly in the Library's Song list or in an album list — and select Add to playlist (see Figure 8.7). Select New and type a name for the playlist. You can then add additional songs to the playlist by long-pressing the song, choosing Add to playlist, and then selecting your playlist.

You can delete playlists you no longer need by long-pressing them in the Playlists section of the Library and selecting Delete. Note that deleting a playlist does not delete the list's songs from your phone.

Figure 8.6
The Lock screen showing the current song; not available on all devices

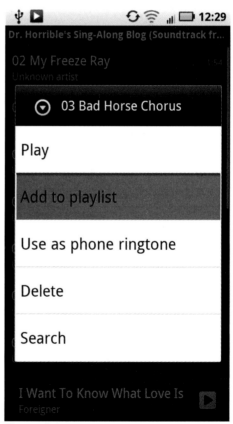

Figure 8.7
Long-press a song to display the menu with the Add to playlist option.

## ALTERNATE APP

Many other applications exist for managing and listening to music on your phone. Two particularly popular apps are TuneWiki and Meridian Player. TuneWiki, which is available in a free, ad-supported version or for purchase for $4.99 without ads, enables you to both play songs on your phone as well as stream tunes from Internet radio stations. The free Meridian Player includes features similar to TuneWiki's, minus the Internet radio. Both are available on the Android Market.

## ADDING A HOME SCREEN WIDGET FOR MUSIC

You can directly access your music and play songs from your home screen by adding a widget. As with other widgets, you can long-press on the home screen, select Widgets or Android Widgets, and then scroll to Music.

The widget displays the song currently playing, as well as enables you to pause the song and skip to the next song in the album or playlist (see Figure 8.8). You can also select the song directly to access the Music app.

## USING SONGS AS RINGTONES AND NOTIFICATION SOUNDS

You can use a song in your library as the ringtone for your phone or for specific contacts. You can also set songs as notifications for operating system events and for some applications. You can set the ringtone to a

**Figure 8.8**
The Music home screen widget

song by long-pressing the song in the library and selecting Use as phone ringtone.

You can also use songs as ringtones for specific contacts so that you can tell when they are calling without looking at your phone. Unfortunately, Android by default does not make this process obvious, as the settings for contact ringtones display only the default system tones and the phone's current ringtone. However, this actually provides a workaround. You need to first set the song you want to use for your contact as the phone's ringtone by following the steps outlined in the previous section. Then, you can open your Contact app, select the contact you want to use, and then press the Menu button and select Edit. Scroll through the contact's details until you see the setting for Ringtone — you may need to select the Additional info bar to see it. Select the Ringtone setting, and you see the song you just set as the phone's ringtone in the list. Select it and then click OK. Obviously, you then need to go back and reset your phone's ringtone.

Although a built-in method to make this easier would be nice, several third-party apps have been developed to solve this problem. One of the more popular is Ringdroid, which is available free in the Market. When you launch Ringdroid, it automatically brings up a list of all of the songs on your phone and includes a handy search to quickly locate a particular song. Ringdroid's primary purpose is to enable you to edit songs to use as ringtones and notifications, so when you select a song in the application, it opens the song in a new screen that shows the waveform for the song with simple buttons you can drag to set the beginning and ending points (see Figure 8.9). After you finish editing, press the phone's Menu button and select Save, at which point you are presented with a dialog box that enables you to name your edited clip and select whether the phone will be saved as a ringtone, a notification sound, alarm, or music. If you choose to save as a ringtone, you then are presented with options to set the ringtone as the default tone for your phone or assign it to a particular contact.

## LISTENING TO INTERNET RADIO

Internet radio stations enable you to listen to a variety of songs, just as you would on a

> ### TIP
>
> Another method of setting notifications and ringtones is to save your songs into a proper folder on your phone. If you connect your phone to your computer and mount it as a USB drive, you can explore its folders. You see a Music folder, which contains the songs and albums you have uploaded or synched to the phone. You also see a media folder, which contains an audio folder that, in turn, contains ringtones and notifications folders. The music player sees the songs in the Music folder, and ringtones and notifications see songs in the media folder. This is why your music player's library is not cluttered with all of the phone's ringtones, but is also why those songs do not appear when you try to set your ringtone or notification. You can copy a song into either the ringtones or notifications folder to have it appear when you set either sound on your phone.

traditional over-the-air radio station. One of the more popular applications to listen to Internet radio is Pandora, available for free from the Market. Pandora enables you to specify artists or genres that you like, and it then plays songs not only from what you specified but from similar artists as well, enabling you to discover songs you might not otherwise know of. When you first install the app, you need to create a new free account with Pandora if you do not already have one.

Once registered, the application asks you for your favorite artist, song, or composer. It

Figure 8.9
Editing a song

Figure 8.10
My Pandora station, based on Foreigner

then creates a new radio station for you with songs from that artist or composer, as well as similar songs (see Figure 8.10). While a song is playing, you can select the thumbs-up or thumbs-down icons at the bottom of the screen to tell Pandora whether you like the song or not. If you vote thumbs down, the song immediately stops and does not play in your station again, but if you vote yes, the current song is used as criteria for picking other songs.

You can press the Menu button on your phone and then the first of the icons on the menu to display a list of your stations. From

here, you can again press the Menu button and select Create Station to specify an artist or song.

## IDENTIFYING MUSIC WITH SHAZAM

Science fiction author Arthur C. Clarke once stated that any sufficiently advanced technology was indistinguishable from magic. Shazam seems to prove him right. With this simply, well, magical application, you can have your phone listen to any music playing, whether on the radio or over the speakers in a store or restaurant, and it will identify the song, displaying the song title and artist and even allowing you to purchase the album.

Shazam is technically a free application, meaning that you can download it without paying. However, the company recently changed the rules for using the application to limit free users to identifying five songs per month. If you think you need to identify more than that, you can purchase a subscription to the service.

After the application is downloaded and installed, the application could not be simpler to use. All you need to do is launch the application and select anywhere on the screen. The app takes a minute or so to listen to the music before displaying the information about the song (see Figure 8.11).

You should note that Shazam will not be able to identify absolutely every song you try. You often cannot use it in very loud situations such as bars, as too much other noise can interfere with its ability to listen to the song. Also, it cannot identify live recordings or performances, and I have noted that it generally has trouble with classical music. Still, despite these limitations, the app is pretty darned amazing.

## DOWNLOADING AND LISTENING TO PODCASTS

A podcast is a nonstreamed audio broadcast, which is the fancy way of saying that it is a recording you can download and listen to at your leisure. The term podcast replaced the original name, webcast, thanks to the rise in people who chose to listen to them on their iPods. Many traditional radio programs are now recorded and distributed via podcast, but a large number of podcasts today are recorded specifically for that medium.

**TIDBIT**

Pandora limits the number of times you can skip a song, regardless of whether you skip by giving the song a thumbs down or just use the skip button. You can skip up to six songs per hour, and if you remain with a free account, you can only skip 12 times per day. A Pandora One account, currently priced at $36 per year, lifts the daily (but not the hourly) limit, along with removing the advertising. You can get more details on subscribing at http://blog.pandora.com/faq//contents/64.html.

The accepted standard for recorded podcasts is to save them as MP3s, and you can treat them as such: You can simply download the MP3, transfer it to your phone, and listen to it using your phone's Music player.

**TIDBIT**

Obviously, Shazam does not actually rely on magic. Rather, it records a sample of the song it hears and submits it to Shazam's servers. There, the recording is analyzed for its "acoustic fingerprint;" that is, it looks for the song's frequency peaks and then compares it to those songs in its database. Although I have encountered many times when it was unable to find a match, I have yet to encounter a time when it gets something wrong.

However, most podcasts are not one-time events; rather, podcasts usually are recorded on some schedule. What really distinguishes a podcast from any other MP3 is that you can subscribe to a podcast and have them downloaded automatically as new recordings become available. Many podcasts are distributed completely free of charge, and others may require a subscription fee.

## Find and Subscribe to a Podcast with Google Listen

In order to subscribe to a podcast and take advantage of automatic downloading,

you need to install a podcast application such as Google Listen, available as usual from the Market. After you have the app installed, you can begin to subscribe to podcasts. Within Listen, you can search for podcasts using the search icon at the top of the screen. After you find the podcast you are looking for, select one of its episodes and then select Subscribe (see Figure 8.12).

You can listen to the current episode immediately. You also can return to the main Listen screen by pressing your phone's Back button several times, and then select

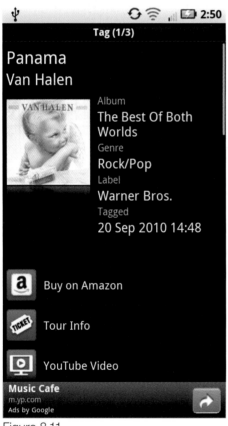

Figure 8.11
A song identified by Shazam

Figure 8.12
Subscribing to a podcast

the My listen items link. This selection displays a list of items you have listened to or are waiting to listen to; select the title of an episode to listen.

## Manually Add a Podcast to Listen

Occasionally, you may encounter a podcast that has not been indexed by Google and so will not display in the search results. Fortunately, you can add the podcast manually using your phone's Web browser. You simply need to go to the podcast's Web site and find a link to the RSS feed for the podcast, which should be somewhere on the home page. Select the link to display a list of the applications you have installed that can handle the feed; click Listen. A screen appears, asking you to confirm that you want to add the subscription, so click Add to launch Listen (see Figure 8.13). The podcast is displayed as if you had searched for it, so you can now select Subscribe.

Figure 8.13
Adding a Podcast subscription

# Taking Pictures

## The Skim

The most-photographed person in the world in the nineteenth century was Gen. George Armstrong Custer. There are around 200 known pictures of him. Even a few decades ago, taking pictures was a costly enterprise. When I visited the Soviet Union on a high school class trip, I took around 300 pictures over the course of two weeks. But that, of course, has changed, quite dramatically, in the last few years: on a recent weekend trip to Disneyland, I took close to 1,000 pictures. This meteoric rise in picture taking can be directly attributed to two factors. First, the fact that digital photography has made individual pictures free. My limit of 300 pictures on the trip to Russia was due primarily to the amount of film I could afford, but to my kids, the very concept of "film" is as outdated as a sundial. Second, and just as important, is the sudden proliferation of cameras. Today, nearly everyone owns a camera simply because nearly everyone owns a mobile phone, and they are one in the same. Good news here: Although early mobile phones included cameras that took less-than-stellar pictures, today's devices contain cameras that rival what you would expect to pay several hundred dollars for in a dedicated camera.

## TIDBIT

As good as the cameras included in today's phones are, they are still in the end point-and-shoot cameras. Most will not allow you to adjust things like f-stop and ISO speeds. (If you do not know what an f-stop is, then you probably don't care that your phone will not allow you to change it, so you need not worry. In fact, you can go ahead and stop reading this sidebar and return to the main text.) Many cameras suffer from slow shutter speeds as well — my old G1 had such a ridiculously slow shutter that it was all but impossible to get a clear shot of anything that was not absolutely still, which is a nice way of saying that it was basically worthless for getting shots of the kids. Only the newest models even include a flash. Although it is certainly nice that your phone includes a camera, keep in mind that it is still first and foremost a phone. If you are really into photography, your phone is not likely to replace your dSLR anytime soon.

## USING YOUR PHONE'S CAMERA

Your phone's camera can be accessed in a number of ways. Your phone might include a button, usually located somewhere along the outside edge, which is used to actually snap the pictures, but also can be pressed to simply launch the camera application, or you can launch it as you would any other application on your phone.

After you launch the app, your screen should display whatever you happen to be pointing the camera at. On some phones,

this is all you will see, but on others, you may have additional controls and options visible on-screen. At its simplest, taking a picture simply involves pointing your phone's camera at the subject and pressing the camera button on the phone. The picture is saved automatically. On some phones, the new picture may appear briefly before you return to the camera view, while on others you will be taken back to the camera view immediately. If your phone includes a flash, it will fire — or not — at the software's discretion.

## VIEWING YOUR PICTURES

The fact that pictures are now free is, as I mentioned, one of the really great things about digital photography. Another great thing is the fact that you can view pictures instantly to see whether you really got the shot you were looking for. My kids take this for granted; every time someone points a camera at them, which is a lot because they are, of course, really cute kids, they expect to be able to walk — or more often run — over and see the picture right away.

Whether your phone's camera displays the image for a few seconds or not, the most recently shot image will display as a small thumbnail in the bottom corner of the camera app while you prepare to snap the next photo. Simply select the thumbnail to display it. Depending on your phone and the exact version of Android you are running, you either get the last photo full-screen, or some other display of your images. On the Droid X, the images appear in the so-called Camera Roll, which allows you to scroll through them with a cool animated effect (see Figure 9.1).

You also can view your photos without going into the camera at all by using the

Figure 9.1
The Droid X Camera Roll

Gallery application, one of the standard applications in all versions of Android. Once again, the exact details of what the Gallery displays varies between models and variants of Android, but the basics are the same: You see your images organized into some sort of folder structure. Usually, the pictures you have taken with your camera's phone will be separate from pictures you may have downloaded off the Web and separate from pictures you may have transferred from your computer. You can select each folder to display its images, and then select any image to display it full-screen.

Most phones automatically rotate pictures as you rotate your phone, so that pictures with landscape orientation will shrink to fit the available space when you hold your phone normally but rotate to display full-screen when you hold your phone sideways (see Figure 9.2). The opposite applies to pictures taken with a portrait orientation.

# SHARING YOUR PICTURES

Any picture you take with your phone can be shared instantly with others, using text messaging, Facebook, Twitter, or other applications.

## Sharing with MMS

Although texting was, as the name implies, designed for text, the system has been expanded to now include the ability to transmit multimedia content such as pictures. Technically, it uses a slightly different technology, known as MMS or Multimedia Messaging Service. Android enables you to very easily add a picture to a text message without worrying about which technology is being used.

If you want to text a picture you have just taken, you can do so directly within the Camera or Gallery app. When viewing the picture full-screen, press the phone's Menu button and then select Share. You

Figure 9.2
Pictures automatically rotate with the phone.

get another menu that lists the applications on your phone capable of sharing pictures (see Figure 9.3); select Text Messaging. A standard text message window will open, in which you can type the recipients to which you want to send the picture and a note explaining it. When done, select Send.

**TIP**

An irony of newer phones is that they often take pictures too large to send via text message. Therefore, you may see a warning that the picture you are sending is too large and needs to be resized. Simply select Resize to have the application do this for you. Do not worry, though, as only the copy of the picture that is being sent is resized, and the original will remain untouched.

## Sharing on Facebook

Facebook originally was conceived as a service built around the idea of sharing pictures, and it has, in fact, become a common way for many people to share pictures of family, vacations, or important events. If you have the Facebook app installed on your phone, it integrates with the Gallery to enable you to easily upload pictures you take with your phone to Facebook. See Chapter 5 for details on installing and setting up the Facebook app on your phone.

To begin, follow the steps outlined in the preceding section to select a picture and display the menu of photo-sharing services. This time, obviously, you want to select Facebook. Doing so launches the Facebook app to the Upload photo section. You can type a caption for the photo and then select

Upload. It may take a moment or two to upload the photo, but after you do, it will appear on your Wall and in the Photos section of your Facebook account.

## Sharing on Twitter

The Twitter service itself allows you to post only short text messages of no more than 140 characters. Pictures and anything else are not supported. However, a number of services have sprung up to enable Twitter users to upload their images and then post a link to the image on Twitter. Many of

the Twitter clients even display the image automatically when viewing a tweet. See Chapter 5 for details on getting started with Twitter on your phone.

To post a picture to Twitter, follow the steps outlined previously to select the picture and display the menu of applications that can share it. This time, select Twitter. The application automatically generates a link on the photo-sharing site Twitpic, which will be inserted into your Tweet (see Figure 9.4). Type any other text you want to add to the tweet — keeping

Figure 9.3
The applications on my phone that can be used to send pictures

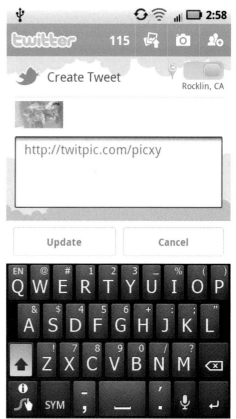

Figure 9.4
Preparing to send a tweet with the link to Twitpic generated automatically

## TIP

Unfortunately, the Facebook app does not automatically rotate your pictures and, in fact, does not provide any means of doing so, so if you have pictures taken in the portrait orientation, they show up sideways on your account. At best, this will be a bit annoying, and, at worst, you might have friends like mine who will rather mercilessly mock you for committing such a faux pas. Thankfully, although the Facebook app does not provide help, you do have ways of editing the picture so that it is rotated properly before you post; read the section "Edit Pictures on Your Phone" later in this chapter for details.

in mind that the entire message, including the Twitpic link, must be no more than 140 characters — and select Update. The picture then is uploaded to Twitpic, and your tweet is posted for all of your followers to see.

## Sharing via E-mail

You can also go old school and simply e-mail a picture to someone. If you have a person who has an older phone that cannot directly accept MMS messages, or perhaps works in an environment that does not allow access to or use of phones, e-mailing remains a reliable sharing model.

Follow the steps outlined previously to select the picture, this time choosing either Email or Gmail as the sharing option, depending on which one you use. See Chapter 5 for details on both. Either way, a

new message is generated with the picture added as an attachment. Simply enter the recipient addresses, a subject, and a message body, just as you would any other e-mail and select Send.

## Other Sharing Methods

Your phone may contain other applications that support sharing photos. For example, the Droid X includes a social sharing application that connects to a number of social networks and enables you to post the picture to multiple networks at the same time. It also includes an application that can connect to certain retail outlets to directly print your images.

## DOWNLOADING PICTURES TO YOUR COMPUTER

In addition to sharing images electronically, you also can download your images to your desktop or laptop computer. To do this, you need to simply plug your phone into your computer using USB. Then mount your SD card by pulling down the Notification Bar and selecting USB Connection. Depending on your version of Android, you are either given a simple dialog box with the choice to mount your SD card, or a more complex one with several options (see Figure 9.5). If you have the former, select the button to mount the card; if the latter, choose either PC Mode or USB Mass Storage, as either will work in this case. See Chapter 1 for a more thorough explanation of these options.

With the card mounted, your computer should automatically detect your phone as a new hard drive. If you use Windows, you are shown a dialog box with a set of options for how to deal with the card. If you have a

Figure 9.5
SD card mounting options on the Droid X

photo-editing or management tool installed on your computer such as Adobe Photoshop Elements, you should see an option to automatically import the photos into it, which is the easy way to download the images. If you do not have a program that can import for you, select the option to open Windows Explorer.

If you need to manually download the images, you can simply use either Windows Explorer or Mac Finder to drag the images from the phone's Albums folder to your hard drive.

# FIND OUT WHERE YOU TOOK A PICTURE

Your phone includes a GPS device. Most of the time, we think of using GPS within Maps to find directions to places, as is covered in Chapter 7. However, many other applications can and do use GPS, including your camera. If enabled, the GPS function in your camera can record the latitude and longitude of every picture you take in a process known as geotagging. How is this useful? Well, it allows you to display a map on your phone of the precise location for each picture, which can be particularly helpful when you are traveling and may end up taking pictures of fairly similar monuments or sites. After you transfer your pictures to your computer, you may have programs that can perform similar functions as well using the geotag embedded by your phone.

## Enabling GPS on Your Camera

Many newer models of phones come with geotagging enabled on the camera by default; this was the case with my Droid X. Other cameras may need it to be turned on. The exact steps needed to enable the geotagging on the camera phone may also vary slightly, but in general they will be located in either the settings or tags sections of the menu. On the Droid X, you can turn geotagging on or off by pressing the Menu button on the phone, selecting Tags, and then either checking or unchecking the Auto Location Tag setting (see Figure 9.6).

When taking pictures on the Droid X, you can tell whether geotagging is on by looking in the top-left corner of the screen when you first launch the camera. If enabled, you will see a small tag icon and, for a few seconds,

121

## TIP

Geotagging on your camera suffers from the same shortcomings as any GPS-enabled application: Your phone must have a clear line of sight to one of the GPS satellites, which in the Northern Hemisphere generally means a line of sight to the southern sky. Thus, pictures taken inside will not generally get tagged, as will other pictures taken when the signal might be blocked, such as downtown in large cities. Also, be aware that your camera and GPS are, independently, two of the biggest drains on battery power, so combining them means that you will lose power much faster than normal if you are taking a lot of pictures.

your current location. If the location has disappeared, you can tap the tag icon to display it again.

## Using Geotagging on Your Phone

After you have taken pictures with geotagging enabled, you can display the latitude and longitude by bringing up a picture in the Gallery and tapping the information icon — the small I in the corner of the screen. This will display details about the image, including the location where it was taken (see Figure 9.7). From the same information screen, you can select the Maps icon to the left of the coordinates to launch your Maps application and see where you took the picture.

## EDIT PICTURES ON YOUR PHONE

For more than 20 years, Adobe Photoshop has been the industry-standard photo-editing tool. The desktop application, while extremely powerful, is unfortunately quite expensive. Fortunately, however, you can now leverage much of the power of Photoshop directly on your phone absolutely free.

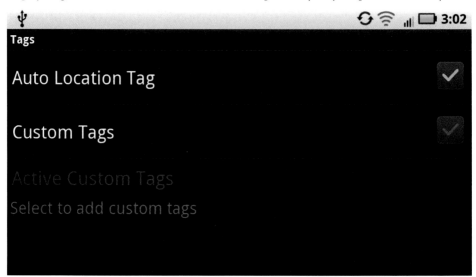

Figure 9.6
Enabling or disabling geotagging with the Auto Location Tag setting

## TIP

Computers are primarily sold by throwing a bunch of numbers at unsuspecting customers, hoping that they will not know or really worry about what those numbers mean. Just about everyone has a vague sense that somehow higher numbers are better. Digital cameras suffer from this as well, but unfortunately, the big number everyone discusses is something of a red herring: megapixels. Walk into any electronics or photography store, and you will hear the word thrown about with reckless abandon, but ask the people in the store — customers and salespeople alike — what it actually means, and you will likely get a bunch of half-mumbled responses that, in the end, all translate to "I don't know." So then, what is it? Well, your computer's display is sort of like a big sheet of graph paper, and each little square on the graph is known as a pixel. Mega is the prefix for a million, so in literal terms a megapixel is a million pixels. How this relates to photography is that every image is a rectangle made up of pixels, so megapixels describe the size of the image: An image that is 1000 pixels wide by 1000 pixels tall would contain 1 million pixels and would, thus, be 1 megapixel. The number of megapixels associated with a camera, therefore, describes the maximum size of image the camera can take. Why, then, did I describe this as a red herring? Well, because ultimately, to quote Yoda, "Size matters not." Lots of megapixels means that you are getting big pictures, but that does not necessarily mean that you are getting good pictures. Two much more important factors govern the quality of images, neither of which has changed in the slightest since the camera's invention roughly 150 years ago: the quality of the optics in the camera, and even more important, the quality of the photographer behind it. Only time and practice can improve the second factor, but consider the first the next time you buy a camera: a 6-megapixel camera with really good optics will beat a 12-megapixel camera with bad optics every single time.

You can download the Photoshop Express application from the Android Market. Once installed and launched, it will display all of the images on your phone (see Figure 9.8).

Choose any image to display it full-screen. Then press your phone's Menu button and select Edit Photo (see Figure 9.9). You can also press the Edit button at the bottom of the app window and then choose the image you want to edit. This will reload the image, this time including a set of tools both above and below.

The first of the tools along the top is the Crop tool. Selecting the tool displays a menu of tools, including Crop, Straighten, Rotate, and Flip. Cropping enables you to cut away areas of the image to either make it smaller or to focus your viewer's attention on some particular part of the image. When you select the tool, you will see the image with a box highlighting the area to be saved. You can drag to resize or move this crop area. The lock icon at the bottom of the screen allows you to maintain the image's aspect ratio as you crop. After you have the area you want to save selected, simply select the green check mark, which returns you to the editing window. You can also select the

Figure 9.7
The information screen for one of my pictures, showing the coordinates at which it was shot

Figure 9.8
Photoshop Express loaded on the phone

red circle with the X to cancel your edits and return to the Edit window.

The Straighten, Rotate, and Flip tools all do exactly what they say. If you take a picture when you are not holding the camera perfectly level, you can use the Straighten tool to correct your mistake. The Rotate tool spins your image in 90-degree increments, which can be helpful if you are planning to upload your image to a service such as Facebook.com that will not automatically rotate pictures taken in the portrait orienta-

tion. The Flip tool flips your photo either horizontally or vertically. As with the Crop tool, you can select the green check mark to apply your changes or the red X to cancel them, each returning you to the Edit screen.

You can make adjustments to the image using the tool to the left of the Crop. Selecting this tool gives you choices for Exposure, Saturation, Tint, Black & White, Contrast, and Brightness (see Figure 9.10). All except the Black & White tool work in essentially the same way, enabling you to drag your finger on the image to either increase or

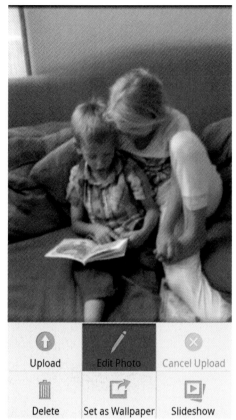

Figure 9.9
Preparing to edit the image

Figure 9.10
The menu of options for editing your image

decrease the effect of the tool. Exposure changes the overall lightness or darkness of the image. Saturation either increases or decreases the amount of color in the picture, and Tint changes the overall colors (see Figure 9.11). Contrast and Brightness, like Exposure, change the lightness and darkness of the image, but whereas Exposure affects the overall image, Contrast only lightens or darkens the shadows of the image, while Brightness affects the highlights. The final tool in the set, Black & White, does what it says: It converts your image to black and white. It does not have any adjustable settings.

The final two top menus apply effects. The first button applies a soft focus filter to your image, which you can adjust by dragging (see Figure 9.12). The second displays a menu with an option to apply other effects and one to apply borders. The effects include filters such as Vignette Blur and Soft Black & White; it is really easiest to simply play with these on images to see the effect. Borders enable you to apply a border such as simple white lines or an old film emulsion look.

The options along the bottom of the screen, from left to right, enable you to

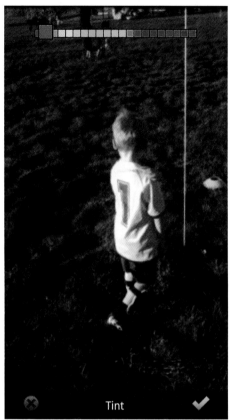

Figure 9.11
Changing the tint of the image

Figure 9.12
Applying the Soft Focus filter

cancel all edits you have made to the image, undo your last edit, redo your last edit, or save the image. A very nice feature of the program is that it always saves your edits to a copy of the image, so you can really do whatever you want to a picture and not worry about ruining the original.

After you complete your editing and either save or cancel, you are returned to the main app screen. From here, you can upload your image to the Photoshop.com Web site, Facebook, or Twitpic, where you can easily share your pictures with others. The Photoshop.com Web site requires that you

create a free account before you can upload images; when you select the Upload button and select Photoshop.com, you are given the choice of either logging into your existing account or creating a new one.

If you have or create a Photoshop.com account, you can access any photos you have uploaded via the Online tab at the top of the applications main screen. You can view these images and set them as your phone's wallpaper, but you cannot directly edit them.

# Video

## The Skim

am an unapologetic film buff. A friend recently asked what I thought was the single worst movie I have ever seen, and honestly, it was a question I could not easily answer. That was not to say that I have not seen any bad movies, but rather, that I have seen far too many bad movies to be able to pick out any one in particular. I really will see almost anything and have on more than one occasion simply showed up at a theater and bought a ticket for whatever happened to be starting next. (He knew he did not need to ask what my favorite movie was, because you need only spend a little time with me to discover my undying devotion to Joss Whedon's *Serenity*. In fact, you do not even need to get to know me, because I do manage to throw at least a few references to the movie or the TV show upon which it was based into every one of my books.) Given this love of film, it should be no great surprise to find that I like shooting video as well. Growing up, video cameras were too bulky and far too expensive to be anything more than a novelty to many, but today, the same factors that have pushed the astronomical rise in still photography have begun to apply to video. Cameras are smaller and cheaper than ever before and have become progressively easier to use. Android phones have, from fairly early on, included the ability to capture video, but many of today's models include cameras capable of capturing video in high definition.

## CAPTURING VIDEO ON YOUR PHONE

Depending on your model of phone and your variant of Android, the exact name of your video application may vary; on the Droid X, it is appropriately enough called Camcorder. You can also access the video camera by going into your phone's regular camera and finding the button, displayed somewhere on the screen, that switches the camera's mode to video.

Either way, once you are in the camera you can simply point and shoot: Press the same button on the camera you use for taking a picture to start recording, and then

**TIP**

Unless you are intentionally trying to shoot video in the style of *The Blair Witch Project*, you should try as best as possible to remain still while shooting. Along the same lines, if you are going to zoom in or out, do so slowly. While underlighting worked well for Ingmar Bergman, you will likely find that the better the lighting in the area you are shooting, the better your movie will look. If your phone includes a flash, you will be able to select the Light button on the camera app to turn on the flash, but be aware that this will cause a significant strain on the battery.

press that same button again to stop. Some models allow you to zoom in and out on the video while shooting. The Droid X uses the volume buttons for this, but instructions on zooming should display on the camera when you first launch it.

You do have a limited amount of time you can shoot. For all the advances in video, one big hurdle remains: video files are huge. Thus, you will find that you can fill your SD card quite quickly if you use the video camera a lot; plan to download the video to your computer frequently. Your device may also impose a limit on each video; on the Droid X, you are limited to 30 minutes per shot.

## VIEWING YOUR VIDEOS

You can watch your movies as soon as you shoot them by selecting the screen immediately after stopping the video and then pressing the Play button (see Figure 10.1). Videos are also available via the Gallery, alongside your photos (see Figure 10.2).

On some newer phones, you may be able to play a video directly on your TV. The Droid X and a few other models include an HDMI jack. If your phone includes the jack and you have a high-definition TV, you can purchase an HDMI cable for your phone from your local electronics store and then plug the phone in and play video.

## SHARING YOUR VIDEO

If you would like others to see your cinematic masterpiece, you can easily upload your video to YouTube from your phone. From the Gallery, select the video to open it, then press the Menu button and select Share. From the resulting menu, select YouTube (see Figure 10.3). You can add a title

Figure 10.1
Play a video by pressing the play button — the large triangle in the middle of the screen.

Figure 10.2
Videos in the Gallery

to your video and select More details to add a location and set the video to either Public or Private (see Figure 10.4). If you select Pub-

lic, the video will appear on the YouTube site for all to see; if Private, only you will be able to view it by logging into YouTube.

Figure 10.3
Sharing your video via YouTube

Once the video has been uploaded, you can continue to view it on your phone via the Gallery or with the YouTube application that comes as a standard part of Android. You can also view it online via the YouTube Web site (see Figure 10.5).

## STREAMING YOUR VIDEO WITH QIK

Qik is an oddly spelled but useful online service that allows you to directly stream

**TIP**

You may not know this, but you already have a YouTube account. Several years ago, Google bought the video sharing service after attempting, and failing, to create a competitor, so the same Google account you needed to create in order to start using your phone works on YouTube.

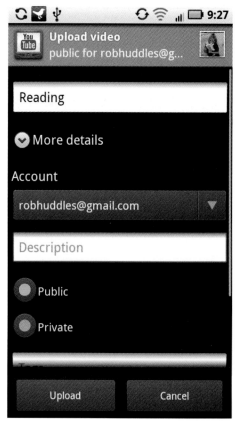

Figure 10.4
Setting the details on the video

video from your phone to Qik's Web site. Using Qik, you can shoot a video of your child's elementary school play and let grandparents in a different state watch live online.

To use this service, you need to download and install the Qik application from the Market, and then set up a free account (see Figure 10.6). You can then start broadcasting your videos right away — simply select Record (see Figure 10.7) and then select the big red button to begin. The address on which others can view the video will display at the bottom of the recording window.

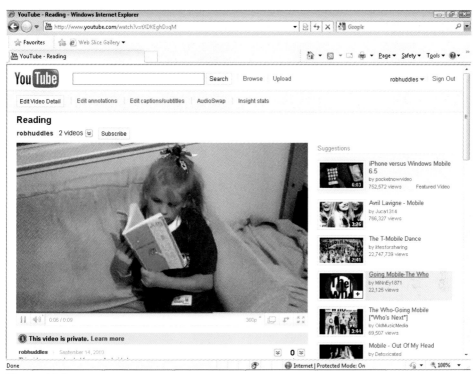

Figure 10.5
Viewing a video shot on my phone on YouTube

Press the Menu button, then Settings, then Sharing to set up preferences for sharing your video with others. You can enter your usernames and passwords to Facebook, Twitter, YouTube, and GTalk to have the service automatically post messages when you broadcast (see Figure 10.8).

## PREPARING A VIDEO TO UPLOAD TO YOUR PHONE

In addition to shooting and watching your own videos, you can also upload videos from your computer to your phone. In order to do this, however, you need to do a few things to the video on your computer first.

Of course, the very first step is to make sure that it is legally okay to convert and

upload the video you are trying to use. In very broad terms, you should be able to transfer videos you purchase or download online to your phone, so long as you do not plan to use that video for any public viewing. Store-bought videos such as DVD or Blu-ray discs, may have additional restrictions, but many newer movies include a digital copy expressly for this purpose. If you have one of those, you can pretty much skip this entire section, because the digital copy will already be all set for transferring to your phone.

Once you are sure you can use the video, you may need to convert it to the proper format. According to Google, Android supports movies in 3GP and MP4 formats, but

133

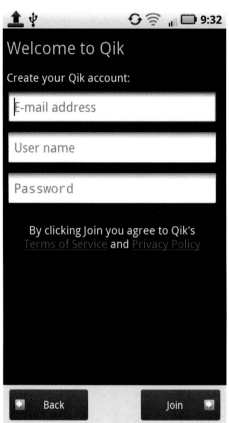

Figure 10.6
Registering for an account on Qik

Figure 10.7
Record and stream a video by selecting Record.

they do include a nice little caveat devices "may provide support for additional formats or file types". Just this week, I dropped an AVI file on my Droid X and had no problems. So there are two bits of bad news here: First, there is a pretty good chance that whatever format your video is in, it will be wrong; and second, there is no easy, sure-fire way to know that. The good news is that you can, fairly easily, convert video from one format to another, albeit with a few caveats. While I cannot say with any certainty what format your particular device does or does not support, I can tell you two formats that

it most definitely will not: DVD and Blu-ray. Technically, neither of those is a format per se, but the point is that you can definitely not expect to put a DVD into your computer's drive and find a file to drag onto your phone and expect it to play. Those you will definitely have to convert, assuming that they are not encrypted. You will need some software on your machine to perform the conversion for you. Here again is good news, as a handy piece of software has been created for just this purpose: Handbrake. It is able to convert video from almost any for-

**Sharing Settings** 🔼 ⚡ 🔄 📶 🔋 9:40

## Facebook
Set up your credentials in your Qik profile.

## Twitter
Set up Twitter account and sharing preferences.

## Youtube
Set up your credentials in your Qik profile.

## GTalk
Set up your Gtalk account to enable sharing via it

## People
Set up personal sharing options

Figure 10.8
Setting up sharing preferences

mat to almost any other format, completely free, and both looks and acts identical on both Windows and Mac. Download Handbrake from http://handbrake.fr/downloads. php and install it. Once complete, launch the program (see Figure 10.9).

Click the Source button in the top-left corner and select the video you wish to convert. If you need to convert a video you already have on your computer into a different format, select Video file; if you are going to try to convert a DVD, select that option. Then select the format into which you wish to convert; remember, for Android you want MP4. Then click the Video tab and select H.264 from the Video Codec drop-down list (see Figure 10.10). Next, go to the Picture tab and change the Anamorphic setting to loose, which will allow you to manually enter a

**TIP**

Handbrake can do a fine job ripping non-copyright-protected DVDs, but what about ones that are protected? And hey, it is the twenty-first century, so how about Blu-ray? Well, Handbrake cannot handle encrypted DVDs without some help, and it cannot deal with Blu-ray at all. It is possible to decrypt copy-protected DVDs, but the legality of doing so, particularly in the United States, is still in the realm of things being argued by lawyers and judges. If you are interested in doing it anyway, there are plenty of resources online to walk you through it. As for Blu-ray: These are the discs where you are likely to find a digital copy, so you may be in luck. If not, you can read instructions for ripping a Blu-ray disc at http://gizmodo. com/5161848/how-to-rip-blu+ray-discs; note the important point the site makes that it takes a very long time to rip Blu-ray discs.

size for the video. Go up to the Width text box just above that and enter the width of your screen; if you do not know what it is, you should be able to look it up on Google by searching on your phone and the words "screen resolution". For example, typing "Droid X screen resolution" tells me that my screen is 480 x 854, so I would set the width to 854 or less — note that you cannot size videos up in Handbrake, so if the width is already less than your resolution, you should leave it at its original size (see Figure 10.11). Finally, click Start (see Figure 10.12). Be

Figure 10.9

Handbrake on Windows; a Mac version is also available and is identical in both look and function. And no, I have no idea what the cocktail glass and pineapple represent.

Figure 10.10

Specifying video settings for the conversion

Figure 10.11
Setting the resolution

Figure 10.12
Starting the conversion

aware that video compression can be very slow, so you will need to be patient.

## UPLOAD A VIDEO TO YOUR PHONE

You can upload videos from your computer to your phone exactly as you would any other file. Plug the phone into your USB port and mount the SD card by pulling down the Notifications bar, selecting USB Connection, and either Mount SD Card, PC Mode, or USB Mass Storage; any will work. Once mounted, your phone will appear on your computer as an additional drive. Navigate to the Video folder on the card and drag your movie there. Then unmount the card by clicking the icon on your task tray in Windows and selecting either Eject or Stop, or on a Mac by dragging the drive to the trash can. On your phone, pull down the Notifications bar and select Unmount. Keep in mind that

video files can be quite large, so you will need to be sure that you have enough space on your SD card for them.

Once you have the video transferred to your phone, you will find it in the Gallery alongside any videos you shot yourself (see Figure 10.13). You can play these videos exactly as you would any other: Simply select it in the gallery to begin playing. A set of playback controls will appear for a few seconds when the movie starts with a pause button and a slider that allows you to move to any part of the movie; you can get these controls back at any time by double-tapping on the screen.

## WATCHING TV ON YOUR PHONE

Several techniques exist to allow you to watch TV shows on your phone. A simple one that works on almost all Android devices is the TV.com application, avail-

Figure 10.13

A movie copied from my computer to the phone appearing in the Gallery able free from the Market. TV.com streams TV shows from its servers. None of it is live TV, and a lot of the content is in fact old shows such as the classic *Star Trek* (see Figure 10.14). Newer content is available from CBS, UPN, Showtime, and a few other networks (see Figure 10.15). Despite its limited content, the application does provide everything for free, so it is nonetheless worthwhile.

Figure 10.14
The "Trouble with Tribbles" is still funny, even on a 4-inch screen

Figure 10.15
Some of the offerings of the TV.com application

# The Web

## The Skim

Few technologies have changed the world as quickly as the Web. While the inventions of the wheel, the printing press, and sliced bread might, in the bigger sense, be more important, none took hold of our collective consciousness as quickly as the Web, which in 2010 was only 20 years old. Equally as interesting is the fact that no one saw the Web coming. In the 1960s, *Star Trek* predicted an impressive array of modern technology, including mobile phones and portable computers, but if you go back and rewatch the whole series, you will never hear Mr. Spock tell Captain Kirk that, rather than asking about the capabilities of that Romulan ship or whether or not that planet is habitable, he could just Google it.

While having the entirety of human knowledge at your fingertips is pretty cool, we were, for most of the Web's existence, limited to looking things up on a heavy desktop computer that was inconveniently attached to the wall via cables. Wi-Fi let us break free of the cables, and now our phones take us a step further, allowing access to the Web literally anywhere.

## SURFING THE WEB ON YOUR PHONE

All Android devices include a browser, which is built on Google's Chrome desktop browser. Most likely, your carrier placed a shortcut to the browser directly on the home screen, but, of course, it is available in the Application Launcher. By default, your home page is a search engine. In many cases it will, not too surprisingly, be Google.

The behavior of the browser varies from one version of Android to the next. On some phones, pages will appear full size, with buttons in the lower corner that allow you to zoom in and out. Newer models contain a browser that displays pages zoomed out by default, so that you can see the entire page at a glance, and then either allow you to zoom in by pressing buttons or, on phones such as the Droid X that support multitouch, allow you to zoom by pinching the screen. You can also zoom in to view the page full size on the page by double-tapping anywhere on the screen, and zoom back out to see the entire page by double-tapping again.

You can navigate to pages in the same way you would on a traditional desktop browser. You can type the address of the site you wish to visit in the address bar at the top of the browser, and then select Go (see Figure 11.1). As you type, you will get suggestions for Web sites that match what you type, both from your favorites and history as well as Google's search. If the site you are looking for appears in the suggestions, you can simply select it to save typing the rest of the address.

## SEARCHING THE WEB

As you are using a device running an operating system made by Google, the fact that you can easily search the Web from your phone should come as no surprise. You actually have a variety of ways that you can perform a search.

Figure 11.1
Opening a Web page by typing its address in the browser's address bar

## Searching the Old-Fashioned Way

Of course, you can use your phone's browser to navigate to Google, type the term on which you wish to search, and choose the search button — the magnifying glass to the right of the search field. This will display the results just as they would on your computer.

## Limiting Search Results

You can limit your search results to a particular region by adding a locale to the search. For example, a search for "pizza" will return millions of results related to all things pizza, but a search for "pizza, San Francisco, CA" will return a list, and map, of the pizza restaurants in San Francisco. A search for "pizza near me" will return a list of the restaurants near your current location (see Figure 11.2). You can limit your search to a specific Web site by including it in the results as well, so a search for "Android" returns a massive amount of sites devoted to Android, while a search for "Android site:wiley.com" returns a much more focused list of books and articles related to Android on this book's publisher's Web site.

Google search can also serve as a calculator by simply typing a mathematical expression in the search box. You can perform unit conversion by typing something like "1 cup in tablespoons", "350 Euros in US dollars", or "78 degrees Fahrenheit in degrees Celsius". Best of all, none of the techniques here is limited to your phone — they all work in Google on the desktop as well.

## Search without Returning to Google

If you are currently viewing some other page on your phone's browser and need to search for something, you do not need to return to Google's home page. Instead, you can press your phone's Search button, which will display the browser's address bar. Type the phrase on which you wish to search and press Go. The browser will send the term to Google and the results page will appear.

## Voice Search

You can also talk directly to your phone to perform a search. Select the microphone icon to the right of the address bar on the

Figure 11.2

Results targeted near your current location

browser to bring up the voice search box, and then say the term or terms on which you wish to search. This will display the results of your search in the Voice Search application, from which you can choose any link to open the page in the browser.

## Search Outside the Browser

Both text-based and voice search are available anytime on your phone, without first launching your browser. From your home screen, you can press your phone's Search button to display a search field into which you can type a search term; pressing the search icon will launch your browser to the Google search results page.

Voice search is available from the same search box; instead of typing the phrase on which you wish to search, simply select the microphone icon and say your search phrase instead. You can also access the Voice Search application directly in your Application Launcher.

A home screen widget for search is also available. Long-press on your home screen, select Widgets or Android Widgets, and then select Google Search. From the menu of search options that appears, you can select either All, Web, or Apps to determine what is searched. Once you have the widget on your home screen, you can type a search phrase or choose the microphone to use Voice Search.

## USE FLASH PLAYER TO VIEW THE WHOLE WEB

Adobe Flash Player is the most-installed software in history, currently residing

on more than 99 percent of all Internet-connected desktop and laptop computers. Its ubiquity has led to its adoption on a wide array of Web sites, from ads to games to video.

That ubiquity, however, applies to traditional computers. Only recently has Flash Player begun to find its way into the mobile space, and Adobe has targeted Android as the first platform on which to push Flash Player. In order to get Flash, you first need to be sure you are running Android 2.2, also known as Froyo. If you are still waiting for your carrier to upgrade you to Froyo, then go ahead and skip this section and come back when it does. If you have Froyo, however, you may still not have Flash, as some carriers use specialized versions of Android that require additional testing from Adobe before they release Player for it. Thankfully, the company is maintaining a Web site, which can be found at www.adobe.com/flashplatform/supported_devices/smartphones.html that lists all of the phones that currently support Player. If your phone is not on the list, keep checking, as the number of phones that support Flash is constantly growing.

If your phone is on Adobe's list, you may have Flash Player already installed, so check your Application Launcher to see if it is there, or simply visit a Flash-based Web site on your phone. If you are on a supported phone but do not have it yet, you can download it, free of charge, from the Market. (You can use the Market as an alternate method of finding out if your phone is supported or not — simply search for Flash Player. If it shows up, then you are all set; if not, well, try back later.)

Once you have Flash Player installed, you do not need to do anything else. Simply use

### TIDBIT

Prior to Adobe's release of Flash Player 10.1 for Android, some Android phones were able to access limited Flash content via the Flash Lite player. Flash Lite was developed in the early days of Web-capable phones. If you are on a phone running Android 2.1, you may be able to download and install Flash Lite, but be aware that many Flash-based sites will not work on Flash Lite.

the browser to visit a page with Flash content and it will appear and work, just as it would on your desktop or laptop computer (see Figure 11.3)

## USING BROWSER WINDOWS

You can have more than one Web page open at a time by using browser windows. You can open a new window by pressing the phone's Menu button while on the browser and selecting New window. This will appear to reload the browser, returning you to your home page, from which point you can either navigate directly to a new site or search again.

You can press the Menu button and select Windows to see a list of all of the windows you currently have open. Select any of them to return to that window, or select the minus to close the window (see Figure 11.4). You can also open another new window from this screen.

You are limited as to the number of windows you can have open at once. On the Droid X, you can only have eight windows.

Figure 11.3
Flash content running on an Android phone

Figure 11.4
The windows currently open in my browser

Be aware that some Web sites open links in new windows by default, so you may have windows open of which you are not aware. Also, if you reach your maximum number of windows and attempt to click a link on a page that opens in a new window, the browser will display an error message. You will need to manually close some of your windows in order to follow the link.

## BOOKMARK SITES

Just as you can on a desktop browser, you can save a reference to a site as a bookmark to make it easy to return to the site later. While viewing a site, you can press the bookmark icon on the browser's address bar. The bookmark icon looks like a small flag with a star on it. Selecting this icon will display the browser's Bookmarks screen, which shows all of your current bookmarks as page thumbnails (see Figure 11.5). The current page will appear in the top-left corner of the screen with the word Add superimposed on it. Select the page's thumbnail, either type a new name or accept the default, and select OK to add the bookmark.

You can also bookmark a page by pressing the phone's Menu button, then Bookmarks, which takes you to the same place as selecting the bookmark icon on the browser's address bar. In addition, you can press the Menu button, then More, then Add bookmark. This will display the same dialog box as before, prompting you to change or confirm the bookmark name. It will not, however, display the Bookmarks screen.

You can navigate back to a bookmarked page by pressing the phone's Menu button, then Bookmarks, to display the Bookmarks screen. Simply select any thumbnail to go to that page.

Figure 11.5
The browser's Bookmarks screen, showing the page I want to add in the top-left corner

The same Bookmarks screen also includes tabs for Most visited and History. Most visited lists the sites you frequently visit, allowing you to quickly return to your favorite sites even if they are not bookmarked. History displays all of the pages you have visited in the last month.

You can get even quicker access to pages by saving them as shortcuts directly on your home screen. While viewing a page, press the phone's Menu button, then More, then Add shortcut to Home.

# CHANGE THE HOME PAGE

While Google's search page provides a convenient starting place, you may decide you would prefer a different page as your browser's home page. You can set a book-marked page by going to the Bookmarks screen on your browser and long-pressing on the desired page's thumbnail, then selecting Set as homepage from the menu that appears.

You can also change the home page by pressing the Menu button, then selecting More, then Settings. Scroll down to the Set home page option and select it, then type the address of the page you wish to use as the home page.

# INSTALLING A DIFFERENT BROWSER

While the default browser from Google is very good, you may decide that you wish to experiment with one of the alternate browsers currently available on the Market. While almost all browsers will display Web pages in basically the same way, other browsers may offer features not found in the default.

## Dolphin

A long-popular alternate browser for Android is Dolphin. If you are running Android 2.0 or later, you can get Dolphin Browser HD from the Market; users running Android older than 2.0 can get a version without the "HD" moniker. Regardless, both are free.

Dolphin browser includes one major feature missing from the default browser: tabs (see Figure 11.6). Tabbed browsing allows you to open multiple Web pages within the same browser window; odds are very good that you have at least seen tabbed browsing

Figure 11.6
The Dolphin Browser showing tabs for navigating to multiple Web sites

before as every major desktop browser has included the feature for several years.

Dolphin also incorporates many more features into the main interface than does the default browser. You can access bookmarks and your most-visited sites by simply swiping your finger to the right, while swiping to the left reveals a toolbar with an option to browse full-screen, hiding both the browser's address and tab bar and the phone's Notification Bar. In full-screen mde, you can swipe down to reveal a menu screen to switch between open tabs.

Dolphin supports the creation of plug-ins by third-party vendors. You can access a list of plug-ins by selecting the puzzle-piece icon at the bottom of the toolbar, then selecting Get more Add-ons. As of this writing, almost 50 add-ons are available, doing everything from changing how you view Web pages to helping protect your passwords. You can also download the plug-ins directly from the Market.

You can also apply themes to the browser to change its overall appearance. Themes are available from the Android Market. Most of the themes simply change the color scheme of the browser to something other than the default green.

## Opera

Opera is an old standby in the desktop browser scene. While most casual users have likely never heard of it, many Web professionals rely heavily on Opera thanks to the fact that in many environments, it displays pages faster than its competitors. Opera offers an Android-based version of its browser, known as Opera Mini, free on the Market (see Figure 11.7).

Like Dolphin, Opera supports tabbed browsing, although it does so through a somewhat unusual interface: Rather than arranging the tabs along the top of the browser like Dolphin and most desktop browsers, Opera bundles the open tabs into a single button in a toolbar at the bottom of the screen, resulting in an experience more like the default browser's multiple windows than a true tabbed browser.

Opera's biggest feature is one which is well hidden but important if you are not on an unlimited data plan. Rather than simply pulling down Web pages, the browser relies

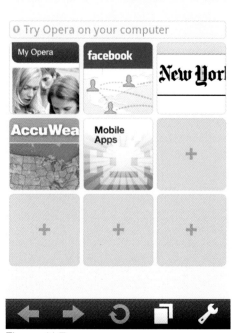

Figure 11.7
The Opera Mini browser

on compression technology that the company claims can reduce your bandwidth usage by as much as 90 percent.

The browser also includes a feature called Opera Link that allows you to synchronize your bookmarks between your phone and your desktop computer, as long as you also use the Opera browser on your desktop.

## Mozilla Firefox

The Mozilla Firefox browser is, by most measures, the second-most popular browser in the desktop world. You may remember the days when Netscape was battling with

Microsoft for dominance in the browser market. When Microsoft won, Netscape was eventually sold off to AOL, which in turn spun the browser development off into an open-source, nonprofit organization that became the Mozilla Project. Fans of Firefox, including myself, have long waited for their browser to find its way to Android, and it almost has. In the summer of 2010, Mozilla released Fennec, the prerelease version of Firefox for Mobile, named for a type of fox found in the Sahara desert (see Figure 11.8). The browser promises to offer many of the features that make the desktop Firefox

browser so popular, including tabbed browsing and support for a plethora of add-ins. It will also offer a synchronization feature similar to that found on Opera and Opera Mini. Keep in mind, however, that as of this writing Firefox for Android is only available as a beta release, meaning that it is still in fairly early stages of development and therefore is likely missing features and may be unstable, which is the polite way of saying that you should use it at your own risk. As a beta release, it is not yet available in the Market, but if you want to give it a try, you can download it from www.mozilla.com/en-US/m/beta.

Figure 11.8
Firefox on Android

# PART III

# Working and Playing

# Documents

## The Skim

W̶e are still some time away from having our mobile devices replace our laptop and desktop computers. I now use my phone as my primary e-mail and Twitter platform, but if I need to create something new, I still need my computer. While creating new documents may not yet be completely practical on phones, reading existing documents, in a wide variety of formats, certainly is here today.

## PDF

In the early 1990s, many users consistently encountered difficulties sharing documents with others, as those documents were more than likely in incompatible formats. Workers at a company that used WordPerfect could not easily exchange information with other workers at companies that relied on Microsoft Word. Adobe created the Portable Document Format, or PDF, as a solution: While the WordPerfect users could not send an editable document to the Word users, they could at least send one that was readable.

Today, format incompatibility, particularly in office environments using word processors, is much less of a concern, mostly due to the total dominance of the market that Microsoft Word now enjoys. Even still, those few offices (mostly in the legal realm) that use WordPerfect no longer have to worry about incompatibility, because for the most part Word and WordPerfect can now read each other's documents. PDF still has a role to play in those situations, but its primary use today is in protecting documents: the very noneditability that was initially perceived as a drawback to the format is now one of its biggest advantages.

For the most part, you cannot create new documents as PDFs. Rather, the vast majority of users convert existing documents into the format. Many ways now exist to do this conversion. You can rely on Adobe Acrobat, but a lot of the software you use on your computer may include the ability to convert to PDF without Acrobat. Microsoft Office 2010 on Windows can convert Word, Excel, or PowerPoint documents to PDF without Acrobat. Creative professionals using the other programs in the Adobe Creative Suite, such as Photoshop, Illustrator, and InDesign, can likewise convert to PDF without additional software. Macintosh users have the ability to convert almost any document on their computer to PDF.

Converting to PDF, however, is only half of the equation: You also need to be able to read documents. Most often, reading on desktop and laptop computers is accomplished via the free Adobe Reader software, although alternate readers do exist. On your Android phone, you have the exact same solution: You can read PDFs sent to you thanks to any one of several dozen PDF readers in the Market, including Adobe's official version of Reader (see Figure 12.1).

You will likely get PDFs on your phone in one of three ways: by clicking a link on a Web site, by having one sent as an e-mail attachment, or by manually copying one to your phone's SD card.

Figure 12.1
Reading a PDF on the phone via the Adobe Reader

## WORKING WITH GOOGLE DOCS

Google Docs is a free, Web-based alternative to a standard office software suite. It includes a word processor, spreadsheet, presentation, drawing, and form application. All documents you create in Google Docs are saved to their servers, meaning that they can be accessed at any time from any computer — or phone — with Web access (see Figure 12.2).

In order to start working with Google Docs, you need a Google account, which,

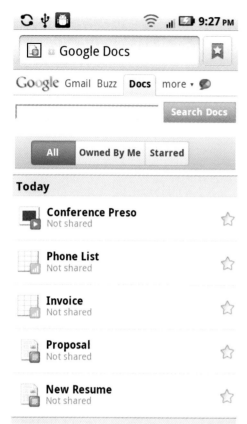

Figure 12.2
The main page of Google Docs, showing the documents I have created

as fully featured as something like Microsoft Word, the Google application allows you to type your document and apply most of the common formatting you are familiar with, such as changing the font, size, and color of text. You can save your document at any time by clicking the Save now button in the top-right corner of the screen, although the application does automatically save for you every few seconds.

You can return to the main Google docs window by simply switching back to its tab in the browser or by closing the document's tab. Selecting Presentation from the Create new button opens Google's alternative to PowerPoint. As with the word processor, you will find many of the basic features here if you are familiar with PowerPoint. The biggest missing feature — the exclusion of which can be considered either a good or bad thing, depending on your views of PowerPoint — is that you cannot apply animation or transition effects in Google's application. You can right-click on items on the slide and select Incremental Reveal to control how text boxes appear on the slide, but that is as close as the application comes to the sorts of effects with which you may be familiar. When in the Presentation application, you will find a Start presentation and Save button in the top-right corner. As with the word processor, presentations are automatically saved on a regular basis.

The main Google Docs window's Create new button also includes an option to create a new spreadsheet, which opens a window and presents an application similar to Microsoft Excel. While again some more advanced features are missing, the basics are all here, including the most important

of course, you already have. You can create new documents on your computer by going to http://docs.google.com. You will need to log in with your Google username and password, at which point you will be taken to the main Google Docs page. On the left-hand side of the page, you will see a Create new button that presents you with a menu of choices of which kind of document you wish to create. If you select Document, a new tab will open in your browser, allowing you to create a document in Google's word processing application. Although not feature for any spreadsheet application: the ability to simplify math through functions. If you are familiar with editing documents and using functions in Excel, you will find the Google Docs version easy to use.

The Google Doc's drawing program is the one in the set that offers the fewest features. If you need to create some relatively simple drawings to accompany a presentation, it might suit your needs, but artists in particular will find it lacking. It functions much more closely to the embedded drawing tools in Microsoft Office programs than a true drawing application.

Finally, perhaps the most unique of the Google Docs applications is Forms, which allows you to create surveys with a variety of question types. Best of all, it automatically records the responses in a spreadsheet, making it easy to analyze the results.

One of the nicest features of Google Docs is the ability to share documents with others. Any document can be shared with any number of users, and you have the ability to control whether those users can edit or merely view documents. In this way, workers at remote sites can have easy access to important documents; one training center I work for with sites throughout California maintains its master class schedule on Google Docs, allowing the managers at each site to view and edit the schedule for all sites.

All of the Google Docs applications are available on your Android device, as the docs are available to any Internet-connected device. Using your phone's Web browser, simply navigate to http://m.google.com/docs. You will likely need to log in again, but then you should see the list of the documents you have created. You can view, but not edit, word processing and presentation documents. Spreadsheets, on the other hand, can be edited to a limited extent: you can alter data in existing cells by selecting the Edit link on each row (see Figure 12.3), but you cannot add more rows or columns to the document.

## WORKING WITH MICROSOFT OFFICE DOCUMENTS

A wide variety of programs exist to allow you to work with Microsoft Office documents on your phone. You should carefully evaluate your needs for an Office application before downloading a free one or purchasing a commercial app. In particular, you should decide if you need merely to be able to read documents, which most of the free apps can accomplish, or whether you need to be able to edit documents, which in general will require that you purchase an app.

### TIDBIT

A few applications exist in the Market to work with Google Docs, but in September 2010 the company announced that it was readying an official application that would allow users to edit and view documents in Google Docs, with the focus on improving security. Unfortunately, the app was not released in time to be included in this book, but may be available in the Market by the time you read this.

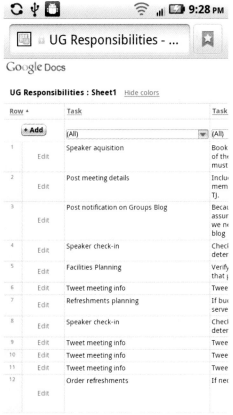

**Figure 12.3**

A Google spreadsheet displaying on the phone. Select the Edit link to alter data.

One such paid app that not only allows you to both read and edit documents but also allows you to create new ones is Quickoffice. Verizon actually bundles Quickoffice with many of its phones, including the Droid X. If you are not a Verizon customer, you can purchase Quickoffice from the Market.

Quickoffice can read, edit, and create new Microsoft Word, Excel, and PowerPoint documents, as well as read PDFs. The application even supports documents created in the newest versions of Office.

## Editing Documents in Quickoffice

In order to edit documents in Quickoffice, you need first to transfer the file to your phone. Perhaps the easiest way to do this is via e-mail; simply attach the document and send or have it sent to an e-mail account that you can access on your phone (see Chapter 5 for details on working with e-mail on your phone.) When the message arrives, open the attachment, which will either open directly in Quickoffice or, if you have more than one application on your phone that can handle documents, you can choose Quickoffice from the dialog box that appears.

You can also attach your phone to your computer and drag documents from your hard drive to your SD card. See Chapter 1 for details. If you choose this method, you will need to open Quickoffice and select Browse from its start-up screen.

It may not be immediately apparent that the document is editable, as Quickoffice does not display any tools, but you can simply choose in the section of the document you wish to edit to place your cursor. Then press the Menu button on your phone, choose Keyboard, and begin typing (see Figure 12.4).

You can apply limited formatting to Word documents by pressing the Menu button and selecting Format. Be aware that an important limitation of the program is that it does not contain an undo function, so if you make a mistake in editing the document, you will either need to manually fix the mistake or close the document without saving changes.

Excel documents function in much the same manner: Either transfer the document to your SD card manually or e-mail it, then open it in Quickoffice. You can double-tap a cell to select it and then type values into the box at the top; unlike with the Word app, the keyboard will automatically appear. Pressing the Menu button gives you access to options to set the number format or switch to other worksheets in the document. You can change the text formatting by pressing Menu, then More, then Font Format. The program supports a full range of Excel's functions, but they must be typed manually into a cell.

PowerPoint documents can be opened in Quickoffice. Initially, you will see thumb-nails of each slide (see Figure 12.5). You can double-tap the slide to zoom in or out, and use the Menu button to switch to a slide show view. The text on the slides can be edited by long-pressing the text you wish to edit and selecting Edit Text. You can only change the text itself; formatting either the text or the slides is not possible.

## Creating New Documents

You can create new documents for Word and Excel in Quickoffice (see Figure 12.6). Keep in mind, however, that entering text

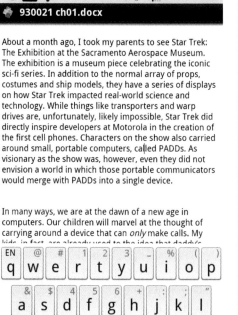

Figure 12.4
Editing a Microsoft Word document in Quickoffice

Figure 12.5
A PowerPoint presentation open in Quickoffice

on a phone, even with Swype, is not as quick or easy — or accurate — as typing on a traditional keyboard, so this capability is unlikely to persuade you to dump your laptop in favor of your phone. Rather, you should see this as a great way to have the ability to create documents on the fly in emergency situations. It may also be useful for certain types of smaller documents such as notes taken during a meeting. Quickoffice does not allow you to create new PowerPoint documents.

In order to edit documents in Quickoffice, you need first to transfer the file to your phone. Perhaps the easiest way to do this is via email; simply attach the document and send or have it sent to an email account that you can access on your phone (see Chapter 5 for details on working with email on your phone.) When the message arrives, open the attachment, which will either open directly in Quickoffice or, if you have more than one application on your phone that can handle documents, you can choose Quickoffice from the dialog that appears.

Figure 12.6
A new document created in Quickoffice. Yes, I really did write the paragraph on my phone.

When you create new documents, you are first prompted to select the type. Unfortunately, Quickoffice is not as clear here as it could be, as your choices are Word Document and Word 97–2003 Document. The app presents a similarly vague set of choices for Excel. What it is really asking is if you want the document to be created using Microsoft's newer file formats — .docx for Word and .xlsx for Excel — or whether you would prefer to use the older formats. The new formats create documents that can only be opened and edited by Office 2007 and 2010, so if you are still using an older version of Office or if you need to exchange the documents with people who are, you should select the older format.

## Other Applications

Quickoffice is not the only app in the Market designed to work with Microsoft Office documents. Another popular application is Documents to Go, which offers a free version for viewing Word and Excel documents, or a paid version that adds PowerPoint and PDF viewing along with editing capabilities.

## READING EBOOKS

Reading books in digital formats is either the best thing to happen to literature since Guttenberg, or the worst. As a devoted reader, I have thus far resisted the temptation to switch to eBooks altogether, although I will admit that the thought of always having something to read — so long as I have my phone with me — is in a way quite comforting.

As with the mobile market itself, the eBook market is for the time being divided into a variety of formats. Thus, you may need several apps on your phone.

One of the more common formats is PDF, which as you have already seen can be read using the official Adobe Reader app or any of the other PDF apps available in the Market. Most likely, you will need to transfer the PDF to your phone by manually copying it to the SD card or via e-mail, although you may also be able to download it directly from a Web site.

**TIP**

It is actually possible to work around the limitation of only being able to read books you have downloaded from Amazon, but it takes some work. Obviously, you should not take this as a license to download books illegally, but there are nonetheless times when you may have a book you acquired legitimately through another source. For example, as the author of the *Adobe Flash Catalyst CS5 Bible*, I was able to get an electronic copy of it directly from the publisher, but as I had not downloaded it from Amazon, the Kindle app was not willing to open it. After doing some digging online, I discovered that the app, quite obviously, only syncs with Amazon's server when it is online. Therefore, you can copy a book you did not download into the Kindle's directory, then turn off both Wi-Fi and 3G, launch the app and read the book successfully. The easiest way to disable Wi-Fi and 3G, by the way, is to turn on Airplane mode. You just need to be sure to move the book's file back out of the Kindle's directory before you go back online.

## Amazon Kindle

Another very common format is that used by the Amazon Kindle. While the company primarily advertises the Kindle as a stand-alone device, it has also created a Kindle app to allow you to purchase and read eBooks directly on your phone. The official Amazon Kindle app came preloaded on the Droid X and is similarly automatically available on other devices, but if you do not have it you can download it free from the Market.

You can only read books that you have downloaded from Amazon's Web site on the app. The company stores your purchase and download history both in the app and on its Web site, and every time you launch it, the app compares the books in its library to those recorded online. Unfortunately, the app's response to finding books it does not recognize is not exactly ideal: It simply crashes, and will not start up again until the offending book is removed.

In order to download books that the app will accept, open the app, press the phone's Menu button, and select Kindle Store. This will launch your browser and display the store, which is organized into categories including bestsellers, new titles, and classics (see Figure 12.7). You can browse by category or search for specific titles.

While most books being published today are available electronically, many older titles have also been converted, and a lot of those are available free of charge. The Kindle Store's main page includes a link to free popular classics, with great works such as Sir Arthur Conan Doyle's *The Adventures of Sherlock Holmes*, Bram Stoker's *Dracula*, most of the works of Shakespeare, and my own personal favorite book, Mary Shelley's *Frankenstein* (see Figure 12.8).

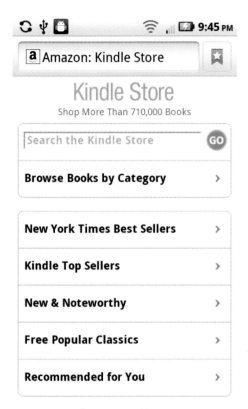

Amazon.com Home

Figure 12.7
Categories of eBooks available in the
Kindle Store

Newer releases almost always cost nearly
as much as the print version. Keep in mind
that the majority of the cost involved in
producing a book is in paying authors and
editors and in real labor costs such as layout, and not the actual printing, so you
should not expect switching to reading
titles electronically to significantly reduce
your book-buying budget. All books you
purchase with the Kindle app are processed
through Amazon, so if you already have an
account you can sign into it on your phone
and use the one-click ordering process,

Letter 1

TO Mrs. Saville, England

St. Petersburgh, Dec. 11th, 17--

You will rejoice to hear that no
disaster has accompanied the
commencement of an enterprise
which you have regarded with
such evil forebodings. I arrived
here yesterday, and my first task
is to assure my dear sister of my
welfare and increasing confidence
in the success of my undertaking.

I am already far north of
London, and as I walk in the
streets of Petersburgh, I feel a cold
northern breeze play upon my
cheeks, which braces my nerves
and fills me with delight. Do you
understand this feeling? This
breeze, which has travelled from

Figure 12.8
Mary Shelley's *Frankenstein*. If you think
you know the story from all of the bad
movies that have been supposedly
based on it, do yourself a favor and read
the actual novel.

which enables you to begin reading a book
within a few seconds of deciding to buy it. If
you do not have an account already, you can
follow the steps outlined in the Kindle Store
to create one.

While reading a book, you can simply
swipe your finger from the right to the left
to "turn" the page. You can also press the
phone's Menu button and choose View
Options to adjust the font size and back-

ground color. The app will automatically remember your spot in the book, although you can manually add bookmarks as you go if you need the ability to return to multiple spots later.

## Aldiko

A popular, free eBook reader for Android is Aldiko. The app comes with Sun Tzu's *Art of War* and H.G. Wells' *The Invisible Man* preinstalled, and includes the ability to download free public domain books as well as free books from a few other sources (see

Figure 12.9). Aldiko only supports books in the ePub format.

Aldiko's only real limitation is that it cannot download books from commercial sites such as Amazon, so you will not be able to read the latest bestsellers. However, if you are more into the classics and lesser-known authors, you will likely not mind the app's selections.

Reading on Aldiko is almost identical to the Kindle app; in fact, if you were just shown a book in both, you would be unlikely to tell the difference (see Figure 12.10).

Figure 12.9
The sources from which Aldiko can download books

Chapter **1**

## Laying Plans

1. Sun Tzu said: The art of war is of vital importance to the State.

2. It is a matter of life and death, a road either to safety or to ruin. Hence it is a subject of inquiry which can on no account be neglected.

3. The art of war, then, is governed by five constant factors, to be taken into account in one's deliberations, when seeking to determine the conditions obtaining in the field.

Figure 12.10
Reading a book in Aldiko

# Games

## The Skim

recently heard someone describe smartphones as a technology that allows users to kill time productively, and thought it an apt description of how I actually use my phone a lot of the time. I will pull it out to quickly check Twitter or e-mail while I am in line at the store or waiting to board a plane. That said, I have to admit that while I use my phone a lot to kill time, it is not always all that productive: There are plenty of times that I will spend time in line playing a game rather than checking e-mail.

The good news for Android users is that the variety of games available on the platform will suit almost any taste. Serious gamers can find games that might rival some found on desktop computers, while more casual gamers like myself can find titles — usually for free — to match our tastes as well.

## PUZZLE GAMES

If you are looking for casual games that you can play in short bursts here and there that will nonetheless require at least some thinking, the Market offers a large selection of puzzle games.

### Andoku

I have an affinity to Sudoku. It is something that you can do a little at a time, and can definitely be challenging. When I got my first Android phone, Sudoku apps were among the first I looked for. I tried out a variety of the free apps on the Market, and by far the best I came across was Andoku (see Figure 13.1). It provides puzzles in five levels ranging from "easy" to "fiendish," with 100 puzzles in each level. All puzzles are timed, and the app keeps track of your fastest and slowest times as well as your average, so you can see if you are somehow managing to get better with each game. The nicest thing about Andoku, however, and what really set it apart from the other Soduko games on the Market was its intelligent input. Too many others relied on the phone's keyboard, which often makes entering numbers slow, while Andoku presents a number pad at the bottom of the screen. Also, it is not ad supported, so you will not find yourself constantly interrupting your game when you accidentally click an ad.

## Traffic Jam Free

Years ago, I was given the game Rush Hour for Christmas. Rush Hour is a simple puzzle game where you take a set of plastic cars and move them around on a board. The goal is to move enough cars out of the way to "free" your car to exit the board. Traffic Jam Free is essentially Rush Hour for Android (see Figure 13.2). The object is the same: You play the yellow car and need to move the other cars, trucks, and occasional limousine out of the way so that you can get to the exit. The game seems almost silly when described, but I think most people will find it fairly addictive. The game's settings allow you to set one of five difficulties, and the free version includes 160 levels. It also contains four themes, including a harbor where you need to free your boat instead of your

Figure 13.1
Andoku, an excellent Sudoku game

car. The commercial version of Traffic Jam removes the ads from the top of the screen.

## aiMinesweeper

Anyone who has ever used a Windows-based computer has almost certainly killed time with Minesweeper. Just in case you have not seen it, it is a simple puzzle game where you are presented with a grid in which you need to find hidden mines without actually triggering them. You do this by clearing spaces that reveal numbers indicating how many adjacent squares contain mines. The game is timed, and those with lots and lots

Figure 13.2
Traffic Jam Free

Figure 13.3
aiMinesweeper

of time to kill at work can get quite good, clearing a 16 x 30 grid containing 99 mines in a matter a seconds. A lot of minesweeper clones exist on Android, but the one that adheres the closest to the original classic is aiMinesweeper (see Figure 13.3). Game play is basically identical to the Windows version; really, the only difference is the fact that the game is green by default rather than gray.

## Tetris

Tetris, invented in 1984 by Russian Alexey Pajitnov, is one of the most popular video games of all time. According to Pajit-

nov's Tetris Company, the game has sold hundreds of millions of copies in its lifetime. An official Android version of Tetris, published by EA Mobile, is available from the Market for $4.99 (see Figure 13.4). This app maintains the game play of the original, but unfortunately lacks what to me was one of the more enjoyable features of the classic game: its soundtrack of Russian folk songs. Instead, the EA game has what could best be described as a techno-funk soundtrack.

In May 2010, the Tetris Company sent a cease-and-desist order to Google demanding that the company remove all Tetris clones from the Market. At the time, Google complied, but as dozens of clones are still available, the ongoing future of unofficial versions of the game remains unclear.

# CLASSIC BOARD GAMES

Google groups quite a few games under its "Brain and Puzzle" category that I would more accurately classify as board games, including classics such as chess, checkers, backgammon, and mancala.

## Chess for Android

While the exact origins of chess are deeply debated, no one questions that people have been playing the game, or at least something similar, for something close to 1500 years. From fairly early on, people have attempted to create computer-based chess games that can provide fun yet challenging game play; in 1997, a computer known as Deep Blue became the first machine to defeat a World Chess Champion when it beat Garry Kasparov. It is no surprise then that the Market is full of chess games, but one of the nicest is titled simply Chess for Android (see Figure 13.5). The app presents a classic, easy-to-view board. It highlights

Figure 13.4
The official Tetris app

Figure 13.5
Chess for Android

the spots to which each piece can move and displays the game's history on the lower portion of the screen. I discovered that not only is the app a great way to play chess, it is also a good learning tool, as I have been using it to help teach the game to my daughter. It contains eight levels, although these seem to relate more to the speed with which your opponent moves than the actual skill of the opponent.

## Checkers for Android

I will admit that I've never been the biggest fan of checkers. I know that there is actually a lot of strategy to the game, and perhaps I just have not devoted enough effort to learning it, so it is still in the range of games I can play somewhat mindlessly. That, of course, means that I can pretty much count on getting beaten every time by my phone's Checkers for Android, made by the same developer as Chess for Android (see Figure 13.6). But the look and feel of the checkers app are very similar to the chess app, including the same levels option that merely slows down the opponent.

## Backgammon

Backgammon is another classic game that has survived for centuries, with sets for a very similar game having been discovered in Iran dating to 3000 BCE. Like chess and checkers, dozens of backgammon games exist on the Market, and the free game simply titled Backgammon is among the best (see Figure 13.7). It contains a very nice, classic-looking board and sound effects of die rolling on wood. One of its more interesting features, however, is an anticheating mode. Backgammon games rely partially on

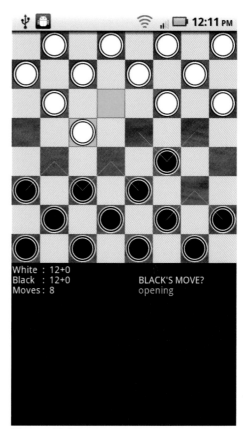

Figure 13.6
Checkers for Android

luck, thanks to the roll of the dice, but also on skill, and skillful players can make moves that increase their chances of being able to capitalize on good rolls while minimizing their opponent's opportunities. Thus, it can often appear as though the computer is cheating by getting better rolls. To prove that this is not the case, the game actually includes an option that allows the human player to roll an actual set of physical dice and input the values, thus bypassing the game's die rolls and proving that you keep losing simply because the game is better than you.

Figure 13.7
Backgammon

## TIP

The only real challenge in finding games to play on your Android device is in trying to choose which ones to download, as the Market is full of thousands of titles in practically every genre. The Market lists games in four basic categories: Arcade & Action, Brain & Puzzle, Cards & Casino, and Casual. Unfortunately, you will quickly come across the Market's biggest limitation: It is designed around the idea of searching for apps, not browsing for them, so once you go into any of these categories you find an overwhelming list of titles, which are presented in a seemingly random order. You could thus spend all of your time browsing for games rather than actually playing them. You might get lucky and stumble upon a couple here and there, but you are unfortunately better off just doing what Google wants you to do in the first place, which is search. Do not search for specific titles, unless, of course, you know the exact one for which you are looking, but instead search on more general subjects, such as Sudoku or hearts or poker. This will generally result in a good list of the titles available for that type of game, which will allow you to find one you like. When evaluating games, I would definitely recommend that you also look at the comments to see what others thought of the title, and remember that all apps have a 24-hour refund policy so if you find a game you think you will like that you have to purchase, you can always try it out and return if it you do not like it after all.

## Mancala

Mancala is not technically a game, but rather a category of games. However, the term has come to be commonly associated with the game Kalah, and the two terms are often used interchangeably, particularly on the Market. The game has its origins in agricultural societies, so many games use the analogy of moving seeds from one pocket to the next, but most modern versions of the game, including the ones you will find in the Market, use instead the idea of moving gem stones. To play, you take all of the stones out of one pocket and place them, one at a time, into the adjacent pockets. You can capture your opponent's stones by counting correctly and ending your turn in an empty pocket. The game ends when all of the pockets from one side of the board are empty. The free app in the Market simply called Mancala is among the nicest available (see Figure 13.8).

## ACTION GAMES

When many people think of video games, they think lots of action and loud explosions. If that is your style, you will find plenty of choices on Android. Unfortunately, few of these games are free.

### Robo Defense

Tower defense games are almost a genre by themselves. These games revolve around the idea of you defending some kind of territory by placing weapons in the path of a seemingly never-ending horde of attackers. You are not responsible for actually shooting your opponents; instead, your guns or other weapons fire by themselves, leaving you to figure out the best placement for your defenses. All of the games provide you with limited resources and defense of varying quality — and cost. While a lot of tower defense games exist on the market, one of the more entertaining is RoboDefense (see

Figure 13.8
Mancala

Figure 13.9). The graphics are a bit too small to make out details, but the idea is that you have to place guns in the path of robots who are attacking what appears to be some sort of fortress. Lower levels tend to be fairly easy, but higher levels become quite difficult. The game is available in a free version with limited maps and levels and a larger, more expansive paid version.

## Angry Birds

On paper, Angry Birds seems like quite a silly game. The story, such as it is, revolves around a group of pigs who have stolen the eggs from a bunch of birds. The pigs have then fortified themselves inside rather poorly made structures of wood, stone, and ice, and the birds have decided to hurl themselves at the structures in order to kill the pigs. Or something. In the game, you take the role of the birds — in each level, you pull back a slingshot and toss birds at

the pigs' structures, which then collapse down on them (see Figure 13.10). You have a limited number of birds, and the object is to kill all of pigs in as few shots as possible. It is unquestionably silly, but also shockingly addictive. Angry Birds is one of the most popular games for Apple's iPhone platform, and now you, too can enjoy it on Android.

## CARD GAMES

Card games are some of the most popular electronic games. From solitaire to hearts to Texas Hold'em poker, you will find plenty of options to keep you entertained if you like playing cards.

### Solitaire

Many solitaire games exist on the Market, including the one simply named Solitaire. This game includes four popular varieties of the game, including regular solitaire, Spider, Freecell, and Forty Thieves. The graphics

Figure 13.9
RoboDefense

are not spectacular, but the game play is fast and very smooth (see Figure 13.11).

Another popular solitaire app is Fun Towers, which essentially reverses the

traditional solitaire game, forcing you to pull cards from the stack back into your hand. It is both simple and surprisingly addictive.

Figure 13.10
Angry Birds

Figure 13.11
Playing Freecell

## Poker

Poker, particularly the Texas Hold'em variety, has become one of the most popular games over the last few years, with ESPN even televising the annual World Series tournament and a plethora of online gaming sites, so it should come as no surprise to see many Android poker apps available. The problem with poker as a video game, however, is that it is very difficult to do well against a computer, because it is a game in which the best hand does not always win thanks to the ability of players to bluff, something that computers cannot easily do nor fall victim to. A few apps exist to solve this problem by allowing you to play live, online against other users. One such app is the Red Poker Club, which can be downloaded for free. You are given a set amount of virtual chips with which to play each day. As with other online poker games, you will find a wide variety of players to match up against.

## GAMES THAT TAKE ADVANTAGE OF YOUR PHONE'S ABILITIES

While the majority of games for Android are games that have existed in other forms and have merely been ported to the phone, a growing number take advantage of the unique properties of your device.

### Graviturn Extended

The object of Graviturn Extended is simple: move red balls off the board while keeping green balls on it (see Figure 13.12). The catch is that you rely on the phone's accelerometer for movement, so you actually need to twist and turn your phone around to move the balls around. As with most games like this, Graviturn gets harder as you go and constantly introduces new challenges, the hardest of which are squares that, when hit by a ball, actually reverse the gravity so that tilting the phone one way

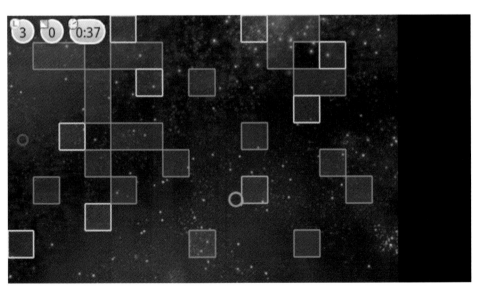

Figure 13.12
Graviturn Extended

causes the balls to move in the opposite direction. Graviturn won an award in the Android Developer's Challenge in 2009, and playing it makes it easy to see why. Best of all, the game is free.

## SpecTrek

SpecTrek is an augmented reality ghost-hunting game. The idea is that you use your phone's GPS system to hunt down ghosts in your neighborhood; when you get close to one, you can tilt your phone up and begin using the camera, which overlays the ghost against the real-world backdrop. You can then choose a net icon on the screen to "capture" the ghost.

The game begins with a warning to play it only on foot, as you will obviously be looking at your phone's screen most of the time, rather than paying attention to what is around you, so operating a vehicle of any kind can be dangerous. You should also be

aware that playing the game in a crowded environment such as a city can be equally hazardous, not to mention that you're sure to get some odd looks from passers-by. A nice open park is probably the ideal place to play.

## WEB-BASED GAMES

Most games available on the Web require Flash Player, which is both good news and bad. The bad news, of course, is that if your phone is not running at least Android 2.2 and supporting Flash Player, then you will not be able to access some online games. The good news is that the number of phones that do run 2.2 and Flash Player is quickly expanding. See Chapter 11 for more details on getting Flash on your phone.

If you do have Flash, then all you need to do to play Flash-based games on the Web is to simply go to the site in question and play as normal (see Figure 13.13). Be aware,

Figure 13.13
Playing a Flash-based game at Orisinal.com

however, that while Flash Player has been optimized for mobile, many sites might not be. If a game requires keyboard input, for example, and your phone only has a virtual keyboard, you may find that the keyboard takes up enough space on your screen that the game becomes all but unplayable. Other games may have problems with simply being too large.

# Other Cool Apps

## The Skim

Stargazing with Google Sky Maps ◦ Finding Local Businesses ◦ Getting Movie and TV Information with IMDb ◦ Creating Shopping Lists ◦ Calculating Tips ◦ Taking Notes with Evernote ◦ Planning Trips with Kayak ◦ Keeping Track of the Weather with WeatherBug ◦ Researching with Wapedia and Wikimobile ◦ Finding Recipes ◦ Following Your Favorite Sports Teams ◦ Scanning Barcodes ◦ Translating with Google Translate

What separates smartphones from regular cell phones, of course, are the apps. Apps are what people want to see when you show them your phone; they are what phone manufacturers focus on in advertising their products; they are how people are making money in the mobile world. Spend enough time browsing the Market and you are likely to find that there is, in fact, an app for that. What "that" is, exactly, depends on your personal taste.

## STARGAZING WITH GOOGLE SKY MAPS

From a very early age, I have been fascinated with the stars and space. Some of my earliest memories, in fact, are of hanging outside with my dad, staring up at the stars. As I got older, I began learning about constellations and the science of astronomy. When Halley's Comet last visited Earth in 1986, my parents bought me a telescope, and I can recall spending many evenings outside looking at the planets and stars. Of course, while all of those years of study gave me a better-than-working knowledge of the sky, I still had to rely on paper and plastic star charts to figure out where things were; many times, it was only when I pointed my telescope at a planet that I figured out which one it was.

A few weeks ago, I got the chance to begin to pass on this obsession to my kids when my daughter's science class learned about the moon, which spurred her to look through my telescope. While we were looking through that same telescope I had when I was younger, gone were the plastic circular star charts. Instead, I had my phone with me outside, and when I wanted to figure out what planet was hanging out near the moon (Jupiter, as it turned out) or find a particular star, I simply opened up Google Sky Maps.

Sky Maps was one of the first apps I downloaded on my old G1; in fact, it was one of my main motivations to get an Android-based smartphone in the first place. Sky Maps is exactly what it says it is. When you

launch it, the app uses GPS or, failing that, triangulation from cell towers to determine where you are, and then presents a map of the sky at that moment (see Figure 14.1). You can identify celestial objects by holding your phone above your head and pointing it at the area of the sky you are looking it.

Sky Maps has a lot of options that allow you to configure what you see. You can simply select the screen to view a menu that allows you to turn on or off sets of objects, including stars, constellations, Messier objects, planets, the Right Ascension and Declination grid, and the horizon.

Selecting the screen also gives you the ability to zoom in and out on the map, and the option to switch between manual and automatic modes. Automatic mode has the map display the objects that the phone points at, while manual mode lets you move around the sky yourself, regardless of the orientation of the phone.

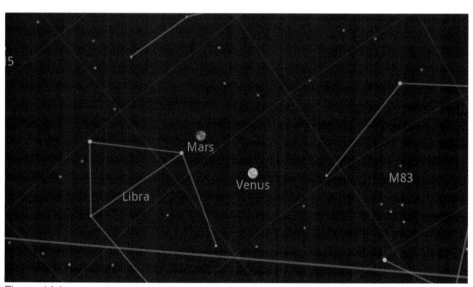

Figure 14.1

Google Sky Maps, showing the current locations of Mars and Venus

You can also press the phone's Menu button to display still more options. Search lets you find a particular object by name or designation. The search will then display a large circle and an arrow; the circle gradually changes color as you move closer to the object, going from blue when you are looking in completely the wrong direction to red and eventually an expanded yellow circle when you find the object. The Menu also allows you to toggle on Night mode, which makes the background black and everything on the display red. Night mode works because your pupils do not expand when exposed to red light, so you can look at the screen and not lose your night vision.

Finally, the Gallery displays a selection of pictures of objects taken by the Hubble Space Telescope. You can select any image to view it full screen, and then select Find in sky to be taken back to the map and shown the location of the object to see it yourself (see Figure 14.2).

## FINDING LOCAL BUSINESSES

The rise of e-commerce over the last two decades has had an undeniably negative impact on smaller local businesses. What used to require a trip to the local independent bookstore or music shop can now be done in the comfort of your own home. Just as important, the Web was not much help for local businesses because finding information on the Web required that users be at home in front of their computers.

The rise of smartphones, however, holds the promise to reverse those losses. Now, you can realistically be out with friends

**TIDBIT**

Charles Messier was a seventeenth-century French astronomer who created a catalog of galaxies, nebulae, and star clusters. Today, these objects are known, appropriately, as Messier objects. The objects are known by a numeric designation Messier gave them; for example, the Andromeda galaxy is M31. There are a total of 110 Messier objects. Nineteenth- and twentieth-century astronomers compiled a much longer list, known as the New General Catalogue or NGC, that includes all of the Messier objects, along with about 7700 additional ones, but most professional and amateur astronomers, not to mention Sky Maps, still use the Messier designations for those in his catalog. One of the things that makes the Messier objects compelling is that Messier himself did not have a very powerful telescope, so all of this objects can be seen with either the naked eye or a relatively small, 4-inch telescope.

and find a good local wine merchant, or track down a hard-to-find rare book that a local used shop happens to carry. Of course, the easiest way to do this is simply use your phone's browser to search just as you would normally, or even start directly from the home screen with the integrated search.

For certain items, a traditional search will work well, but for many others it will not. Unless you live in a very small rural area, a search for local restaurants is not likely to

Orion Nebula

Back to gallery        Find in sky

Figure 14.2
The Orion Nebula in the Sky Map
Hubble Gallery

be terribly helpful, as you will simply get too many results. If you are in a large city, even narrowing down that search by the type of food you want to eat will still likely give you too many hits.

Thankfully, several apps exist on the Market to help you narrow things down. Two popular ones are Where and Yelp. Best of all, both are free.

## Where

Where is a local directory designed to get you to local business quickly. When you start the app, it will determine your location based on your cell provider's network, which is generally less accurate than GPS, but in this case being a block or two off really does not matter. The app's main page displays a set of categories. From here, you can access everything from the weather, movie showtimes, traffic reports, news headlines, and more.

One of Where's most useful categories is Restaurants. This displays a list of restaurants organized by type of cuisine, so it lets me know, for example, that there are unfortunately no Cuban restaurants near me, but more pizza places than you can imagine (the city I live in is known for having an unusually high concentration of pizza restaurants, for reasons no one can quite determine). You can select a restaurant from any of the categories to view its details. From here, you can select Map to display the restaurant's location, or choose its phone number to call for more information or, if necessary, make reservations.

Where's Places directory, accessible from its main screen, lets you find businesses in one of 16 categories: Restaurants, Bars & Clubs, After-Work Bars, Cheap Eats, Lounge, Pool Table, Singles Bar, Romantic Dining, Nightlife, Grocery, Food, Bakery, Hotels, Shopping, Trave,l and Spa & Beauty (see Figure 14.3). Each of these categories displays a list of businesses, and just as with restaurants, you can select any business to get details, location, or to call it.  Each business and restaurant contains reviews written by other users and an overall star rating, letting you tell at a glance whether the place is well liked or hated by other locals.

Another useful feature of Where, also accessible from its main screen, is its Events category, which displays music, performing arts, sports, singles, food, and family activities in your area. These are a great way to figure out what to do on a lazy Saturday afternoon or to get acquainted with an area new to you.

Another great feature of the application is its ability to look up nearby gas prices. You can select the grade of fuel you prefer, and the app will display gas stations within 10 miles that carry that type of gas and how much they currently charge, letting you

know that you can save 10 cents a gallon by driving an extra mile.

## Yelp

Yelp serves much the same purpose as Where by providing a localized directory of businesses and services. It has fewer categories on its home screen, but if you select the Nearby icon, then one of the categories such as restaurants, you will see that it ultimately has about as much information as Where (see Figure 14.4). Like Where, Yelp relies heavily on user reviews, and displays star ratings on initial

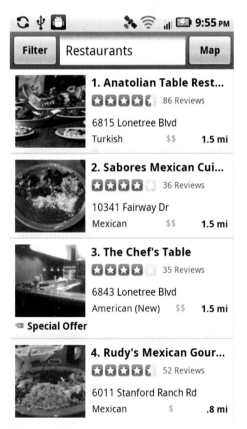

Figure 14.3
The Where Places categories

Figure 14.4
Yelp's local restaurant view

listings and detailed reviews on business pages.

Yelp has less time-sensitive information; for example, it does not display current gas prices or events, but in general has more in-depth business directories. It also allows you to filter the lists based on price or, a particularly nice feature, by businesses that are currently open.

It also has one very cool feature Where lacks: the so-called Monocle view. Select this from the main Yelp page, give it a moment to determine your location, and then hold your phone in front of you to see a listing of the restaurants in that direction, displayed on an overlay of your phone's camera view. Buttons along the bottom allow you to switch the overlay to bars or to everything.

## GETTING MOVIE AND TV INFORMATION WITH IMDB

As I mentioned earlier, I am a very big movie buff. Many years ago, I actually got into Web design because I wanted to build a film review Web site. As I began working on the site, I needed a quick way to look up details on the movie, such as the names of the director or stars. I do not recall exactly how I discovered the Internet Movie Database, or IMDb, but it quickly became my go-to site for details. It is without question the only site I have continued to visit regularly for the entire time I have been using the Web.

IMDb was created off of a collection of lists on a Usenet discussion board about movies. Over time, the list grew to the point that it became impractical to merely view it, and on October 17, 1990, one of the people maintaining the list, Col Need-

ham, released a set of scripts that could be used to search the list. By general agreement, this date is considered the birth of the IMDb. In 1992, it became one of the earliest Web sites. The organizers incorporated in 1996, and in 1998 the company was purchase by Amazon, which continues to operate it as a private subsidiary. Today, IMDb is one of the most-visited sites on the Web and contains information on practically every movie or TV show ever produced.

In 2010, IMDb launched its app for Android, which gives users an easy way to access all of the data on the site. I still use it primarily for the same thing I have always used the site for: to quickly look up the names of people in movies and TV shows I am watching. It is particularly helpful to find the name of that actor in the show you are viewing who you recognize but cannot quite place. You can search the app by pressing the phone's Menu button and selecting Search, or more directly by pressing the phone's Search button.

A key difference between the Web site and mobile app, however, is that the app also displays local movie times. From the app's main page, simply select US Showtimes to see a list of the movies currently playing in a theater near you. Each movie lists its running time and the local theaters in which it is playing (see Figure 14.5). Select the film's title to go to the IMDb page about the movie, including a link to the trailer, which you can watch directly on your phone, or select the list of theaters to go to the page that displays the exact showtimes.

Several other apps provide movie listings, including both Where and Yelp. However,

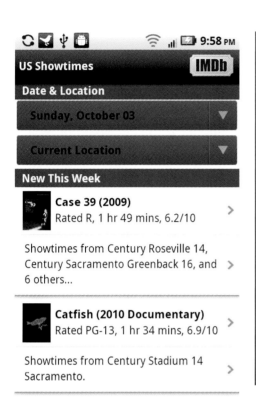

Please be courteous to those around you and stay off your phone while you actually watch a movie. That said, there is one other app you might consider putting on your phone, specifically to have as a reference during the film: Runpee. This app, which provides the information from the Runpee. com Web site, gives you a list of the moments in a movie in which you can run to the bathroom without missing anything important. It tells you when the scene occurs, how long you have, and a description of what you will miss. One of its nicest features is that it also lets you know which movies have extra scenes following the closing credits.

Figure 14.5
The IMDb app showing local movie listings

none provides the amount of detailed information about the movie itself as IMDb.

## CREATING SHOPPING LISTS

We all know the importance of using a list when shopping. Budgeting experts will tell you that you should have a list to avoid wasting money on impulse items, but the real reason is because you will likely forget something without one, and, of course, Murphy's Law says that whatever you forget will be an item that you simply cannot do without, forcing you to make a second trip.

Thankfully, quite a few apps exist on the Market to allow you to create a shopping list directly on your phone. My personal favorite is OI Shopping list. The OI in the name stands of Open Initiative; unlike most of the other apps on the Market, this one has been created by a group of people as an open-source application.

The application is incredibly simple, as a shopping list app should be. You can simply launch the app and begin entering products to create your list. While at the store, simply select the check mark next to each item as you pick it up to know that you have it in your cart (see Figure 14.6).

Press your phone's Menu button and select Clean up list to remove all checked items in preparation for your next trip to the store. You can also select Settings, then Sort order to change the way in which the items

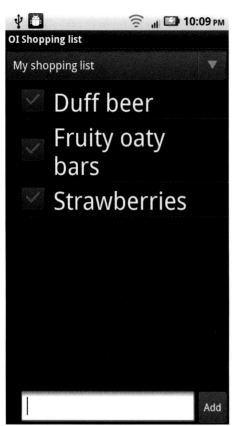

**Figure 14.6**
OI Shopping list in action

as you type new items, so the next time you need to get eggs, you should only need to type "e" and then select eggs from the list that appears.

The app also supports a few cool optional add-ons, the best of which is the OI Barcode Scanner, which allows you to scan the barcode on a product to add it to your list.

## CALCULATING TIPS

Occasionally, restaurants will print suggested tips directly on the bill, but most of the time you are expected to calculate the gratuity in your head. I suppose some people are naturally good enough at math to be able to do so in their heads, but for most of us, you can get a rough approximation of 15 percent, but nothing more. While you could use the calculator that comes built in with Android, a dedicated tip calculator makes things easier.

Tip calculators are another popular category for apps. While the Market does not display the number of apps returned for a search, doing a search on Tip Calculator brings up a seemingly never-ending list of apps, ranging from free to several dollars. After evaluating a variety of the free ones, my personal favorite is the Nerdy Tip Calculator by LucanaTech (see Figure 14.7).

Beyond the fact that I like the name, the Nerdy Tip Calculator is nice because it is one of the few free apps that makes every field editable. Many others do not allow you to manually enter the tax amount. I am not exactly sure when I would need to do this, but it feels nice to have the option.

I also like it because it is again one of the few apps that allows you to split the bill among the people in your party. It will not help if each person is paying only for his

are sorted. I prefer the option unchecked first, alphabetical, which moves each item to the bottom of my list as I check it off.

If you prefer a bit more detail on your list, you can long-press an item and select Edit item to bring up a screen that allows you to enter quantity and price. You can also add tags to items, so, for example, you can tag milk and eggs as dairy, while you tag pineapple and grapes as fruit. You can then sort on these tags to see items that are likely to be close to each other in the store.

The app remembers any item you add, and presents you with an autocomplete option

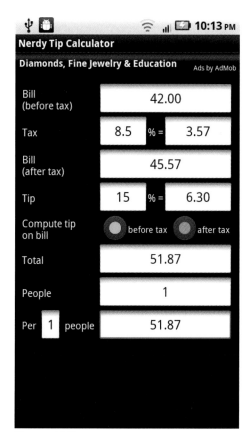

Figure 14.7
The Nerdy Tip Calculator

or her food — the stock calculator is likely your best bet there — but if you plan to split the bill evenly, this tip calculator will work well for you.

## TAKING NOTES WITH EVERNOTE

I was first introduced to Evernote while attending a conference when a woman next to me noted I was taking notes in Word and recommended that I try Evernote instead. At that time, Evernote existed as an online service and a desktop application. The idea is that you can take notes

with the desktop application, but that those notes are automatically synchronized online, giving you access to them from any other Web-based computer. I tried it out at the conference and was quickly convinced as to its utility.

I love the ability to access notes from anywhere, and I use Evernote for all kinds of things: frequent flyer numbers, lists of the movies I have seen or books I have read, Wi-Fi access codes, people who help me out while I write books and need to be thanked in the acknowledgments and more. The only thing missing for some time was the ability to get all of this on my phone. Yes, I could access the Evernote Web site, but it tended to be pretty slow on the phone and was not easy to read. I was thus thrilled when Evernote finally released an app for Android.

In order to use Evernote, you first need to sign up for an account. The company offers both a free account and a paid account that gives you additional storage space online. You can sign up online or within the app. When you log in, you are given four options to get started: you can take a picture of something to save as a note, upload a text file, or start a new text or audio note (see Figure 14.8). You can also search for an existing note by typing a search phrase in the box at the top of the screen. You can also press your phone's Menu button and select Notes to view all of your existing notes. The desktop and Web versions of Evernote rely heavily on tags to organize your notes. In the mobile app, tags can be considered in searching, but are not as obviously used elsewhere.

The only major limitation with the Evernote app is that unlike the desktop version,

Figure 14.8
The Evernote app

present me with a single location that I could use to look up flight details, rental car reservation numbers, and hotel addresses. This is again a category of apps that is fairly common on the Market, and something again that I evaluated a variety of apps without discovering any one that suited my needs. That is, until a friend recommended Kayak.

I was familiar with Kayak as a flight search tool: You can visit the Web site, enter your home and destination cities, and get a list of the cheapest flights between them. However, until I checked out the mobile app, I had never looked at the rest of the features the company offers. Now I use Kayak not only to find flights but also keep myself organized while traveling.

When you open the app you are presented with a set of options, allowing you to search flights or for hotels or rental cars (see Figure 14.9). I have used the flight search on occasion, but generally find the full Web interface to be a lot easier to use, although I can imagine a situation where I might use it for an emergency.

What I find particularly nice is Kayak's Trip feature, which is the travel organization tool I was looking for. Once you create a free account with Kayak, you can store your flight, hotel, and rental car information on its servers, accessing the details from the Web or within the application. What is really cool, though, is that you do not need to manually enter any of these details. Today, just about every travel-related business will e-mail you purchase confirmation receipts. All you need to do is forward these e-mails to trips@kayak.com and within a few minutes, the details will appear in your trip. The service is intelligent enough to

the mobile version does not keep a copy of your notes on your phone. While this is certainly by design, as phone storage still tends to be limited, it does mean that you will be completely unable to access your notes if you find yourself someplace with no 3G or Wi-Fi connection.

## PLANNING TRIPS WITH KAYAK

I do a lot of traveling for work, and needed an app that would allow me to keep travel arrangements organized. In particular, I hoped to find an app that would group related details together into a single trip, even if you send receipts separately.

## KEEPING TRACK OF THE WEATHER WITH WEATHERBUG

I am not a weather geek. Most of the time, I have a vague idea that it is hot or cold outside. However, there are plenty of times when it helps to have a bit more information. It is not a good idea, for example, to let the kids go to school in T-shirts and shorts when it is going to be 50 degrees and raining. It helps when packing for a trip to have an idea of the weather where you are going.

WeatherBug is a great app whether you are like me and need some general info about the weather now and then or if you are a hard-core weather geek. When you launch the app, it will display local weather information: the current temperature, wind speed and direction, and today's high and low temperature (see Figure 14.10). It also displays today's forecast, along with the forecast for the next five days.

The app's real power is in its additional features. Along the bottom of the screen

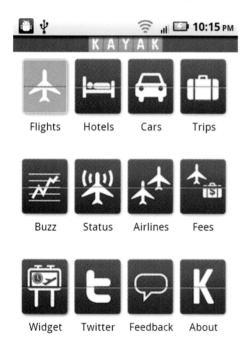

Figure 14.9
Kayak's main screen

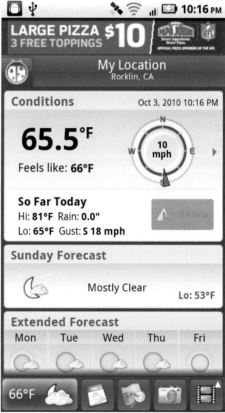

Figure 14.10
WeatherBug's main page

you will find a set of extra buttons. The first takes you to the main page and always displays the current temperature. The second button gives you a more detailed seven-day forecast; you can select any day to get more information. The third of the buttons at the bottom displays live weather radar for your area, while the fourth displays images from a variety of local weather cameras. The fifth and final button loads videos from the WeatherBug Web site, which give you weather information around the country.

You can press your phone's Menu button and select Location to add new locations to the app, helpful if you are traveling or just want to keep up to date on the weather someplace else. Also on the menu is an option for Preferences to change temperature displays to Celsius or to add the current temperature to your phone's Notification Bar.

## RESEARCHING WITH WAPEDIA AND WIKIMOBILE

Several dozen apps exist that give you quick access to Wikipedia, not counting, of course, using the browser to simply access the Web site directly. The two that are fastest and most user friendly are Wapedia and Wikimobile.

Wapedia's interface is clean and easy to use, and the app tends to load articles quickly. Articles in Wapedia are laid out vertically, pretty much exactly as they are on the Wikipedia Web site, so you can quickly scroll through to find the information you need (see Figure 14.11). Press the phone's Menu button and then select the first option to jump to the article's contents. The title of the article displays the number of pages

the article contains, so you have a good idea at the beginning of how long the article is. Unfortunately, there is no easy way to get to the additional pages without first scrolling to the bottom of the current page, but besides that Wapedia is an excellent app.

Wikimobile is another excellent app for accessing Wikipedia. Articles load as pages that you read left to right, which can often be an easier way to read but unfortunately means that you occasionally have to wait a moment while the next set of pages loads. The good news is that you get to watch the

Figure 14.11
Wapedia accessing the Wikipedia article on Android

app's cute dog-chasing-its-tail animation, so all is not lost. The app does not load images from the article by default — a big part of why articles load quickly — but you can use the phone's Menu button to turn on the option to load images if you want. Unlike Wapedia, Wikimobile also does not attempt to remember the last page you viewed.

## FINDING RECIPES

I am always on the lookout for new recipes, and the Favorite Recipes app is a great way to discover new things to cook for dinner. The app has dozens of categories, and its search feature brings up a random selection of recipes for each matching phrase. There are no pictures accompanying the recipes, but the directions are laid out nicely and best of all, each of the recipes I have tried from the app has been very good.

For recipes of a different sort, check out Cocktail Hero. While not an exhaustive cocktail library — it says it contains 260 recipes — its best feature is its "Make It Mode," where you can check off the items you have in your liquor cabinet and it will tell you what cocktails you can make from those.

## FOLLOWING YOUR FAVORITE SPORTS TEAMS

If you are a sports fan, you can use your phone to keep up with your favorite teams. It is no real surprise that the best free app for tracking sports scores comes from none other than ESPN. Its ScoreCenter app displays a wealth of information about ongoing and past games. You can set favorite teams in baseball, basketball, cricket, football, ice hockey, rugby, and soccer, and have access to all of the major leagues within each sport.

The app defaults to showing you the scores and information for these favorites, so you get the information you want quickly without having to wade through a bunch of data you do not need or care about.

My favorite feature of this app is its Home screen widget, which displays the upcoming game for each of your favorite teams (see Figure 14.12). You can scroll through your teams using the small arrows to the left of the widget, and each team's next game displays at the bottom. While a game is in progress, the widget automatically updates to display the current score.

Figure 14.12
The ESPN ScoreCenter widget

# SCANNING BARCODES

You can use your phone's camera to scan barcodes on a variety of products. A wide variety of applications can use this data to show you details on the product.

The basic barcode scanning application is called simply Barcode Scanner, by ZXing Team. Using this app, you can scan QR codes on Web sites to install applications, as is discussed in Chapter 2. You can also scan the barcode on the backs of books and many other products, which you can then use to search the Web for details on the product. This is an app that should be on everyone's phone.

Another app that uses the camera to scan barcodes is Amazon's app. When you launch the app, you have an option from the main screen to search using barcodes. When a barcode is recognized as being from a product Amazon sells, the company's detail page about the product will display (see Figure 14.13). You can purchase the product immediately from Amazon from here, or, the way I more frequently use it, you can add the product to your Amazon wish list in the hope that someone else buys it for you.

Key Ring is yet another great app that relies on scanning barcodes. This ingenious app lets you scan the barcodes on customer loyalty cards. It then saves a high-resolution picture of the barcode from the card. You can then stop carrying the actual card, and instead have the clerk at the store scan your phone. You need to be sure that your phone's screen is clean, but most of the time this will work without issue. The app does display the membership number on-screen, so if scanning does not work the number will be there for the clerk to type in manu-

Barcode scanned: Oct 03
Matching product found:
ActionScript: Your visual blueprint for creating intera...
**$29.91**

More Options

Barcode scanned: Oct 03
Matching product found:
Master VISUALLY Dreamweaver CS4 and Flash...
**$29.19**

More Options

Barcode scanned: Oct 03
Matching product found:
HTML, XHTML, and CSS: Your visual blueprint for designin...
**$19.79**

Figure 14.13
Amazon's detail page, generated from scanning barcodes on the books

ally, ensuring that you still get credit for your purchase.

# TRANSLATING WITH GOOGLE TRANSLATE

Science fiction has long had solutions that allow characters to communicate with others who speak different languages, from Star Trek's Universal Translator or The Hitchhiker's Guide to the Galaxy's Babel fish. While it does not yet know Klingon, the Google Translate app brings you close to making this fiction reality.

When you open Google Translate, you can enter a word or phrase and select to translate to and from any of 53 languages. The app will display the word in the chosen language, but what is particularly cool is its ability to actually speak the word by selecting the speaker icon (see Figure 14.14). In order to use the spoken translation, you need to have the Text-to-speech Extended app installed as well. Fortunately, Google Translate will automatically prompt you to install Text-to-speech when you first launch if it is not already installed.

Figure 14.14
Google Translate

# Advanced Topics

## The Skim

For most users, understanding how to work your phone, take pictures, and install and run apps will be enough. Others, however, will want to do more. You can fine-tune your phone's power settings to get more time between charges, or use your phone to get your computer online. With the Android Software Development Kit, you can back up applications and take screenshots. Finally, if you want complete control over your phone, you can root it.

## MANAGING YOUR PHONE'S POWER SETTINGS

Battery life has gotten significantly better on the latest generation of smartphones, and it will presumably continue to improve. That said, no one can deny that smartphones will drain their battery far faster than a normal mobile phone. While a non-smartphone user can go days or even weeks between charges, you will likely need to plan to keep your smartphone plugged in as much as you can; most cannot go for more than a day or two between charges, and if you use things like GPS or the camera, you will get much less than that.

A variety of apps exists to help you improve battery life. On some phones, Android 2.2 will include a battery manager application by default in the phone's settings, accessible by pressing the Menu button from the home screen.

The Battery Manager displays a large icon showing your battery's current remaining power, along with a set of battery modes. Three modes exist by default: a Maximum battery saver that stops synching data after 15 minutes regardless of the time and dims the display, a Nighttime saver that stops syncing at night but leaves data sync on during the day and does not affect the display brightness, and Performance mode, which leaves all settings alone and in essence does nothing to preserve the battery.

You can also set up a custom mode, where you can define exactly what hours should have automatic synching, how long the phone should wait until it stops synching, and your desired display brightness (see Figure 15.1).

If you do not have Android 2.2, you can download one of the many power management apps from the Market. When I had the G1 and before my Droid X upgraded to 2.2, I relied on Power Manager from X-Phone Software. The free version of the app has a set of profiles preconfigured to progressively dim the screen as power got lower. It would also begin to disable features such as GPS when the power reached a certain threshold. The commercial version of the application, which only costs $.99, allows you to configure your own profiles.

You can also help manage power by paying attention to GPS and Wi-Fi settings, both of which can drain your power. Most apps that require GPS will automatically turn it off as soon as you leave the app, either to return to the home screen or go to a different app, but if you ever notice that the GPS indicator is showing on the Notifications bar when no app is open that should

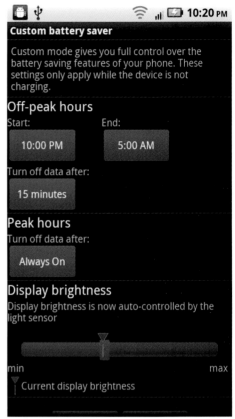

Figure 15.1
Setting up a custom battery saver mode on the Droid X with Android 2.2

be using it, you should be aware that you may be draining your power unnecessarily. Keep in mind that some apps, such as Navigate, will keep running, and keep using GPS, even in the background.

I use Wi-Fi on my phone all the time when I am home, as it is almost always faster than a 3G connection, but then I also have my phone plugged in, either to the wall or, more likely, the computer when I am home. Wi-Fi is another power-hungry service, so if you cannot keep your phone plugged in most of the time, you might think about not using it.

# GET YOUR COMPUTER ONLINE WITH YOUR PHONE

A recent sit-com episode revolved around a character who had moved in with his father. The son, a writer, needed to be online, but the older father did not see the need for the Internet. I can fully relate with the son — I hate having to be off-line. Unfortunately, I still encounter situations where I cannot get online easily. I sometimes teach at facilities that, for security purposes, do not allow me to connect to their network and do not have guest Wi-Fi networks. Incredibly, I even teach regularly at a technology school with no Wi-Fi. As a traveler, it has been a long time since I have been at a hotel that does not provide Internet service, but many hotels charge exorbitant fees to get online, and most hotel networks are painfully slow.

Fortunately, I can now get my computer online with my phone, using a variety of methods. The first, official method is to use the Verizon Hotspot utility. Obviously, this only works if you have a phone running on Verizon's network, and even then Verizon does not support it on all of its phones. For those phones that are supported, such as the Droid X, it is a very easy process: Simply launch the Mobile Hotspot tool that came preinstalled on your phone, agree to the terms of service, and connect. The downside to this method is its cost: Verizon currently charges $20 per month on top of your existing service charges. The big advantage is that this turns your phone into a true mobile hotspot, so other machines besides yours can connect as well if you allow them. Other carriers offer similar services along the lines of Verizon's, and likewise vary based on which phones they support and how much they charge, but an additional monthly charge is the industry standard.

Fortunately, there are several free alternatives. If you have a laptop with a Bluetooth connection, you may be able to connect your computer to your phone via Bluetooth and then use the phone's 3G connection to get your computer online. The exact steps necessary to enable connecting via Bluetooth vary greatly depending on your phone, your version of Android, and your laptop's operating system, but if it can be done with your combination of hardware and software, you should be able to find details online.

PDANet, an app available in the Market, provides another alternative. The app is very simple to use. Install it on your phone, and then install a companion piece of software on your laptop, available from www.junefabrics.com/android/. Once both programs are installed, you can plug your phone into your computer via USB, then enable sharing in the app on your phone. Finally, turn on the connection by simply clicking the Connect link in the program on your computer and you will be online.

PDANet is available in a free version that provides a fully featured trial, after which the app blocks connections to secure Web sites but continues to work on nonsecure sites. The full version, which allows connections to secure sites, is available for purchase.

Another alternative is Proxoid, which sets your phone up as a proxy server for your computer. Proxoid is free, but requires a considerable amount of setup on your computer, all of which will need to be undone when you return to a normal connection.

Thus, it can be helpful for long trips but is impractical if you need to frequently switch between having your computer connected to home or work and connecting via your phone. Proxoid is available in the Market, while details on the necessary setup on your computer are at http://code.google.com/p/proxoid/. Using Proxoid also requires that you have the Android SDK installed; see the following section for details.

# DOWNLOADING THE ANDROID SDK

A Software Development Kit, or SDK, is a package of tools provided by the developer of the language for programmers to use when creating applications. The Android

SDK can be downloaded for free from Google at http://developer.android.com/sdk/index.html (see Figure 15.2). Even if you do not plan to build Android apps, having the SDK installed on your computer allows you to do a variety of other things such as take screenshots of your phone and manually back up its data.

After you download the SDK, unzip it into a folder of your choosing on your computer. Then open the folder and double-click the SDK Setup file. If you want to install the complete SDK, which will allow you to have its full functionality, select Accept All on the Choose Packages to Install screen, then click Install Accepted. Be aware that this might take a while — I have a fast Internet

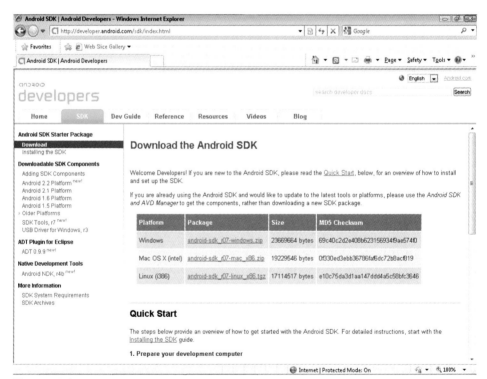

Figure 15.2
The Android SDK page

connection and a fast machine, and this installation took about 15 minutes.

After you have the SDK installed, you will also need to install the Java SDK, also known as the JDK. Java is the language on which Android is built, so you cannot do much without it. Visit www.oracle.com/technetwork/java/javase/downloads/index.html and download whichever the most current version of the JDK is.

If you plan to actually begin working on developing Android applications, you will also need a tool in which you can write your apps. The recommendation from Google is to use Eclipse, which is a very powerful open-source development environment. You can download it from www.eclipse.org, but as this chapter is not about actual Android development you can skip that if you want.

## TURNING ON USB DEBUGGING

In order for your phone to communicate with the tools in the SDK, you will need to enable USB Debugging. This is a very simple process: On your phone, simply go to the home screen, then press the Menu buttons and select Settings. In Settings, select Applications, then Development, then select USB Debugging. You will get a warning message about how debugging is only for development purposes; select OK. You will now see an extra indicator on your Notification Bar. In Android 2.2, this is the Android mascot with extra legs so that it looks like a bug.

Your next step in getting your phone set up with the SDK is the part that I had the most troubles with, and from reading online forums I was clearly not alone. You need to have the proper drivers installed in order for your phone to fully communicate with the

**TIDBIT**

All of the images from the phone in this book were captured by copying and pasting. I use Adobe Photoshop, which has a very handy feature whereby if an image exists on the clipboard, selecting File, then New automatically creates a new document that is the size of whatever is on the clipboard. Images from the Debug Monitor will be at your phone's native resolution; for the Droid X, that is 854 × 480 pixels. I did not manipulate the image in any way in Photoshop; instead, I was using it simply to get the images into the TIFF file format requested by the publisher. I actually created an action in Photoshop to further simplify this process. If you are interested in reading more about how I did this, you can read about it on my blog at www.robhuddleston.com.

SDK. Hopefully, as soon as you plug your phone into your computer, it will detect the device and display a notification about finding drivers. The operating system should fail to find the right drivers, so it should ask you to manually install them, which you can do by going into the usb_driver folder in the SDK.

When I first attempted to do this with the Droid X on Windows 7, it did not work, and eventually I needed to go download new Droid X drivers online. After upgrading to Android 2.2, I again ran into problems, which I eventually worked around by turning USB Debugging off when I need the phone in PC Mode and turning it back on when I need to work in USB Mass Storage mode.

# TAKING SCREENSHOTS

When I first began work on this book, I knew I would need to learn how to take screenshots of my phone, but I thought it was something that authors and bloggers needed to do but would be of very little interest to anyone else. I was therefore surprised by how often it comes up on forums and even in people asking me how to do it. I am not sure exactly why so many people want to do it, but fortunately once you get the setup done it is a fairly easy process.

The simplest method of doing screenshots is via the oddly named Dalvik Debug Monitor, one of the tools in the SDK. Once you have the SDK installed and all of the proper drivers working, you can launch the moni-

tor by going into the folder into which you unzipped the SDK, opening the tools folder, and double-clicking ddms.bat. This tool will open to the Dalvik Debug Monitor, which will show your phone. If your phone does not show up, go back and ensure that the proper drivers are installed. Also, make sure that your phone has USB Debugging enabled.

If you interact with your phone while plugged into the monitor, you can see a fairly constant set of information scrolling across the bottom. Everything happening on your phone is being monitored and reported, which is useful for developers but mostly unintelligible to everyone else.

When you are in the monitor, select Device, then Screen Capture. This will open

Figure 15.3
Capturing an image off the phone

a second screen, which after a moment should display your phone (see Figure 15.3). This is a static picture of your phone; if you change anything on the phone, you will need to press the Refresh button to update the image.

From here, you can click Save to save the image to your hard drive in the PNG format. If you need higher-quality images or require other formats, you can instead click Copy to place the image on your clipboard. Then you can open an image-editing tool such as Adobe Photoshop, paste the image, and work with it from there.

# Index

## • H •

## • U R L s •